THE
GOSPEL OF
THⵔMAS
FOR AWAKENING

THE
GOSPEL OF
TH⊕MAS
FOR AWAKENING

A COMMENTARY ON JESUS' SAYINGS
AS RECORDED BY THE
APOSTLE THOMAS

BY
SWAMI NIRMALANANDA GIRI
(ABBOT GEORGE BURKE)

PART OF THE DHARMA FOR AWAKENING COLLECTION

LIGHT OF THE SPIRIT
PRESS
CEDAR CREST, NEW MEXICO

Published by
Light of the Spirit Press
lightofthespiritpress.com

Light of the Spirit Monastery
P. O. Box 1370
Cedar Crest, New Mexico 87008
www.ocoy.org

ISBN-13: 978-1-7331643-4-4
Light of the Spirit Press, Cedar Crest, NM

Library of Congress Control Number: 2015903151

Bisac Categories:
REL006710   RELIGION / Biblical Studies / Jesus, the Gospels & Acts
OCC012000   BODY, MIND & SPIRIT / Mysticism

08162023

TABLE OF CONTENTS

INTRODUCTION TO THE GOSPEL OF THOMAS

From the very beginning there were two Christianities. One was the Christianity we know today that developed in the Mediterranean world over the centuries. It accommodated itself to the current religious beliefs–especially those of the Roman emperors–and even absorbed and conformed itself to them to such an extent that after three centuries it became the state religion of the Empire presided over by the unbaptized and blatantly unchristian "Saint" Constantine. He was only the first in a series of "vicars of Christ" (this expression originated with the Byzantine emperors and was taken up by the Bishop of Rome) who ruled over the Church as well as the state, and who, despite their often shockingly violent and immoral lives were declared saints of the state servant-church. Today this Christianity is divided into thousands of warring and warlike sects, a multi-headed monster.

The other Christianity was the religion learned by Jesus from his Essene family and during his "lost years" in India, then brought by him back to the "West," to Israel. (See our publication, *The Christ of India*.) Rejected and martyred for teaching that religion, after his resurrection he returned to India and lived thirty or more years at peace in the Himalayas. The Apostle Thomas eventually followed him to India. After some years

Saint Thomas went to Ephesus to be present at the death of the Virgin Mary, then journeyed on to Israel and persuaded a large number of the Qumran Essenes to come with him into South India (the present-day Kerala) to practice the religion Jesus had taught (virtually in vain) to the Israelites. They agreed and did so, linking up with a vast number of Brahmins who had emigrated from Kashmir after becoming disciples of both Jesus and Saint Thomas. It is this Christianity that is found in the Gospel of Thomas.

In December of 1945, an Egyptian farmer near Nag Hammadi unearthed in his field more than fifty ancient Christian books, written in the Coptic (ancient Egyptian) language. Among them was the book now known as *The Gospel of Thomas*. Portions of three Greek copies of the Gospel of Thomas had been found about half a century before in Oxyrhynchus, Egypt. They are known as Oxyrhynchus Papyrus 1 (Oxy P 1), probably written not much later than the year 200; Oxy P 654, which can be dated to the middle or end of the third century; and Oxy P 655, dated not later than A. D. 250. The complete (Nag Hammadi) version in Coptic can be dated to about 340 A.D. The Coptic version is believed to be a translation of the Greek version.

According to the *Pistis Sophia* (Codex Askewianus), after his resurrection Jesus instructed Philip, Matthew, and Thomas to set down his words in writing. While Saint Thomas was in Israel visiting the Qumran community, Saint Matthew gave him a copy of his Gospel, and perhaps at that time Saint Thomas gave Saint Matthew a copy of his record of Jesus' sayings which became copied and circulated among those of gnostic inclination. Since the Nag Hammadi discovery we now possess Saint Thomas' complete Gospel. The translation I will mostly use in this commentary is that of Thomas O. Lambdin.

The traditional "St. Thomas Cross" as found in
Churches in India that trace themselves back to
St. Thomas the Apostle.

THE OPEN SECRETS

These are the secret sayings which the living Jesus spoke and which Didymos Judas Thomas wrote down.

This is the sentence before the Gospel of Thomas actually begins.

Secrets?

Everyone loves secrets, especially children—and those whose brains but not their hearts have matured. Religion is riddled with "secrets," "secret knowledge," "secret practices," "secret fraternities," "secret books," and suchlike, all creating an atmosphere reminiscent of old Flash Gordon serials and the Wizard of Oz. With many it is a passion to be of the elite and know the secrets the commoners know not; to seek and find what only the special few can access; to possess secret knowledge that gives secret *power*....

But Jesus, like Buddha, made it clear that he had no secret teachings, saying: "There is nothing covered, that shall not be revealed; and hid, that shall not be known. What I tell you in darkness, that speak ye in light: and what ye hear in the ear, that preach ye upon the housetops" (Matthew 10:26, 27).

In my search for the real teachings of Christ, I came across a number of secret Christian esoteric associations, all with secret knowledge and secret practices. The interesting thing was that although those groups did possess power and methods that produced an effect, in the final analysis they were ineffectual, and in some cases actually ran counter to the result desired. And in no instance was there the slightest justification for anything they knew or did being kept secret. Jesus certainly knew best, and acted accordingly.

No secrets

"Jesus answered him, I spake openly to the world; I ever taught in the synagogue, and in the temple...; and in secret have I said nothing" (John 18:20).

"No man, when he hath lighted a candle, covereth it with a vessel, or putteth it under a bed; but setteth it on a candlestick, that they which enter in may see the light. For nothing is secret, that shall not be made manifest; neither any thing hid, that shall not be known and come abroad....No man, when he hath lighted a candle, putteth it in a secret place, neither under a bushel, but on a candlestick, that they which come in may see the light" (Luke 11:16, 17, 33).

"Wherefore if they shall say unto you, Behold, he is in the desert; go not forth: behold, he is in the secret chambers; believe it not" (Matthew 24:26).

The forgoing statements are surely sufficient to establish that Jesus had no secret teachings, whatever may be said at the present day. Why, then, this statement about "secret sayings which the living Jesus spoke?" Actually they were not secret, but unknown to those outside the circle of Jesus' disciples. Then they were shunted aside by those who were intent on making Christianity in their own and the "Christian" emperor's image. (It is my speculation that the great library of Alexandria was not burned to destroy "pagan" books abhorred by the official Christians, but to destroy early Christian books no longer compatible with their new state Christianity.) Those that still believed the original teachings of Jesus were forced to keep them secret to escape banishment from the empire, imprisonment, or even death. So the copyist prefaced the book with this sentence, obviously not from Saint Thomas.

Secret/hidden

One English translation out of many–Grondin's–renders the expression "hidden words." The Greek work *kruptos* (from which we get the words crypt and cryptic) means something that is concealed or hidden because it is *inside*–inward. The sayings of Jesus are still secret as far as the outer world is considered because their understanding is a matter of personal, private experience that by its nature remains hidden. And let us not forget another Greek word, *mystikos*, which also means inward and hidden. So we could validly say that these words of Jesus about to be given us are Mystical Sayings.

FINDING IMMORTALITY

And he said, Whoever finds the interpretation of these sayings will not experience death. (1)

Ironically, in the Bible the only verse that approximates this is a quotation from Jesus' enemies: "Thou sayest, If a man keep my saying, he shall never taste of death" (John 8:52).

What is death? Perhaps the best brief definition comes from *Vine's Expository Dictionary*, where life is defined as "conscious existence in communion with God," and death as "conscious existence in separation from God." Since it is impossible for even an atomic particle to be separated from the infinite, omnipresent God, obviously what is meant is that life is *consciousness* of union with God and death is *loss* of that consciousness–the illusion of separation from God. Neither of these have anything to do with the condition–life or death–of the body. Rather, life and death are states of consciousness.

Finding

Jesus said that death will not be experienced by "whoever finds the interpretation of these sayings." This immediately brings to mind the well-known statement of Jesus: "Seek, and ye shall find" (Matthew 7:7).

The Greek text uses the word *zeteo*, which means to earnestly desire and work toward something–it is practical as well as theoretical, and even has the minor meaning of *needing* what is sought. The important word, of course, is *heurisko*, which not only means to find, but has the secondary ideas of both perceiving and possessing the object of the search. So to find the meaning of Jesus' mystical sayings is to inwardly perceive the reality of their meaning and to attain the state of consciousness on which they are based. It is like a rabbi who was an expert in interpreting the Jerusalem Talmud. When asked how he understood it so well, he replied: "Because I know the Source of the Jerusalem Talmud."

Instead of "finds" the Patterson and Maeyer translation of these introductory words has "discovers" and Johnson's has "uncovers." Both of these bear out the interpretation that Jesus is telling us to gain for ourselves the states of awareness which are embodied in these sayings.

SEEKING IS MORE THAN JUST FINDING

Jesus said, Let him who seeks continue seeking until he finds. When he finds, he will become troubled. When he becomes troubled, he will be astonished, and he will rule over the All. (2)

Let him who seeks continue seeking until he finds. For some reason, in reading over the above verse there popped into my mind a memory of the old Dragnet television show. During one episode a woman whose son had become a dangerous criminal whined to Sergeant Friday: "God knows I tried." With his usual dry aplomb Friday retorted: "Yeah, but how hard did you try?" That question applies to these words of Jesus. It is not mere seeking that ends in finding, but *effective* and *prolonged* seeking. Jesus is being a bit like Humpty Dumpty in *Alice in Wonderland* when he told Alice: "Begin at the beginning, and when you come to the end, stop." Just keep going until you reach the goal. Very simple and often very hard to do.

Yet we must grasp this necessary fact of spiritual life: "He that endureth to the end shall be saved" (Matthew 10:22).

Sri Ramakrishna told this parable: "Go forward. A wood-cutter once entered a forest to gather wood. A brahmachari said to him, 'Go forward.' He obeyed the injunction and discovered some sandal-wood trees. After a few days he reflected, 'The holy man asked me to go forward. He didn't tell me to stop here. So he went forward and found a silvermine. After a few days he went still farther and discovered a gold-mine, and next, mines of diamonds and precious stones. With these he became immensely rich."

We, too, have to keep going forward, further and further, "from glory to glory" (II Corinthians 3:18), until we reach the supreme goal–for that alone is what we should be seeking. *We must never stop the search.* It has been said that the desire for God is the way to God. Those who slacken or stop have slacked or stopped in their desire for God. Where, then, is the possibility of finding?

When he finds, he will become troubled. Johnson has "bewildered" rather than "troubled," and Patterson and Maeyer have "disturbed." But others concur with Lambdin in rendering it "troubled."

We read in the book of Acts that Saint Paul and his companions were once described by their religious enemies as "these that have turned the world upside down" (Acts 17:26). We have lived for entire creation cycles in complete delusion. Only now, after more years than human mathematicians can calculate, has a glimmer of reality entered into our purview. And the result? It has seemed to disrupt–if not actually shatter–our life! Look at how people agonize over a very little spiritual insight. In the West it is to the point of absurdity and often insanity. I am not speaking of theory and speculation–Westerners love such mind-games. I am speaking of the sledgehammer impact a few grains of practical truth–for that is what reality *is*–has on everyone's life. It is easy to forget, so maybe you may not recall what it was like the first time reality "struck" in your life. But if you will sit and look backwards you will see that every advance in true knowledge has necessitated a real struggle and perhaps even pain in bringing your life into conformity to it. If not, it still lies ahead for you.

Spiritual history is filled with accounts of people who when given a vision of the truth of things were devastated and disoriented. For never again could they go back to where they were the moment before the lightning struck. Many have foolishly wished it had not taken place. When Sri Ramakrishna opened the consciousness of Naren (the future Swami Vivekananda), his reaction was to weep bitterly and ask: "What have you done to me?" Such is the power of ignorance over our hearts. Like long-caged birds we fear freedom. Many people become upset and even angry when something occurs to open their understanding and make them see more clearly than they did before. What should be a cause for rejoicing becomes a matter of regret and complaint—such is the extent of our spiritual insanity.

It takes great courage to face truth and rise to the level it requires. Before reaching the human form, consciousness evolves blindly, automatically. But humans are on a different plateau, and although they may be forcibly faced with higher reality, they have to agree to it and move up on their own volition. In time they must come to consciously and willfully evolve themselves through the cultivation of inner life. They must become yogis (I mean this in the broadest sense, for every valid religion has produced ways to cultivate higher spiritual consciousness.) Without yoga, spiritual life can be nothing but haphazard, however sincere and devoted the seeker may be.

Even men and women of great wisdom have trembled and shrunk back at the dawning of higher vision, for such vision means a death of much that has heretofore flourished in the twilight world of half-knowledge—much that we have fostered and increased through ages, identifying with it and dominated by it. It is excruciatingly painful to acknowledge that our wisdom has been folly, our living has been death, and our faith has really been only superstition.

When he becomes troubled, he will be astonished. But when the leap is made, when the truth has been not only seen but assimilated into our consciousness, great wonder will arise within us. Lambdin uses the term "astonished," but others prefer "marvel," "amazed," and "wonder." It is said in India that Shiva, the divine yogi, usually sits in profound samadhi in total communion with his Self. But occasionally he emerges from that state and dances in bliss, exclaiming: "O! Who I am! Who I am!"

To enter into hitherto unknown and undreamed-of dimensions of consciousness is a delight and blessedness unthought of by those yet to open those doors of the spirit. Just as the hem of Jesus' garment flowed healing virtue (Matthew 9:20; 14:36), so even the borders of the inner kingdom flow with a glory impossible to describe–but very easy to experience. I well remember the joyful awe that I lived and breathed daily when, after finding the path of yoga I began moving toward the dawning Light. It was something I could never have imagined possible, something undreamed of by the murky religion in which I had been brought up. At last I had found the real gospel (good news) of "Christ in you the hope of glory" (Colossians 1:27). Light had come to me from the East, just as it had to Jesus, and earlier to the Essenes through Moses and Aaron.

Yes, if we can hold firm and bravely move on into the new territories opened by the inner sight, we will be astonished from day to day. Expanding awareness terrifies and panics the ego, but it rejoices the spirit. Many turn back to the ego's realm, but others hasten on into the world of freedom in spirit. Perseverance becomes no longer a trial, but a happy anticipation. "For I reckon that the sufferings of this present time are not worthy to be compared with the glory which shall be revealed in us" (Romans 8:18).

However, the order of things is never changed: first comes the troubling and then the wonder. We cannot have the second without the first.

And he will rule over the All. Jesus is not speaking to us of some kind of abstract intellectual delight or marvel, but of something eminently practical. "Then shall the King say unto them on his right hand, Come, ye blessed of my Father, inherit the kingdom prepared for you from the foundation of the world" (Matthew 25:34). The kingdom of God, the kingdom of heaven, is the limitless expanse of that infinite Consciousness that is God. Those who persevere to the end shall enter into the essential life of God, for "the saints of the most High shall take the kingdom, and possess the kingdom for ever, even for ever and ever" (Daniel 7:18). "And the kingdom and dominion, and the greatness of the kingdom under the whole heaven, shall be given to the people of the saints of the most High, whose kingdom is an everlasting kingdom, and all dominions shall serve and obey him" (Daniel 7:27).

Jesus spoke of this attainment when he told Saint John: "To him that overcometh will I grant to sit with me in my throne, even as I also overcame, and am set down with my Father in his throne" (Revelation 3:21). The identical status which Jesus attained shall be attained by all who seek, find, become troubled and become astonished. They, too, shall rule over all.

"Let this mind be in you, which was also in Christ Jesus: who, being in the form of God, thought it not robbery to be equal with God.... Wherefore God also hath highly exalted him, and given him a name which is above every name: That at the name of Jesus every knee should bow, of things in heaven, and things in earth, and things under the earth; and that every tongue should confess that Jesus Christ is Lord, to the glory of God the Father" (Philippians 2:5, 6, 9-11). That this shall be said of each one of us is indicated by the words of Jesus: "Verily, verily, I say unto you, He that believeth on me, the works that I do shall he do also; and greater works than these shall he do" (John 14:12). The Kingdom shall be our kingdom, the Power shall be our power, and the Glory shall be our glory. Amen.

SEEKING THE KINGDOM REALISTICALLY

Jesus said, If those who lead you say to you, See, the kingdom is in the sky, then the birds of the sky will precede you. If they say to you, It is in the sea, then the fish will precede you. Rather, the kingdom is inside of you, and it is outside of you. When you come to know yourselves, then you will become known, and you will realize that it is you who are the sons of the living father. But if you will not know yourselves, you dwell in poverty and it is you who are that poverty. (3)

Spiritual leaders?

The first problem the seeker encounters in spiritual life is lack of spiritual guidance. The second–and usually even worse–problem is when he gets spiritual guidance. This is no joke. If "it is a fearful thing to fall into the hands of the living God" (Hebrews 10:31), what is it to fall into the hands of incompetent or dishonest spiritual teachers and "gurus"?

I have to confess that I am continually appalled at the thought of what will happen today to the soul that decides to take up meditation or find a teacher of spiritual life. Like a reverse of the radio ads for Ivory Soap that I heard as a child, the entire situation is "ninety-nine and forty-four one-hundred percent" *im*pure. In Chinese Buddhism they speak of the unlikelihood of a blind sea turtle surfacing directly beneath a floating log, and that is about how unlikely it is to receive competent spiritual instruction, especially in meditation. Bamboozled by the razzamatazz of the hawkers in the meditation market, people wander for decades in futility and confusion. Few find the way, particularly in the West, not that those who travel East manage much better. I do not even give thought to those who only want to learn intellectual "truth." Their wandering and hopelessness is guaranteed by their very interest. That is why Sri Krishna tells Arjuna in the Gita (6:44) that a person who simply inquires about yoga goes beyond the scriptures.

Soul friend

In medieval Europe the expression "soul friend" was used for a spiritual advisor. How much better this is than the teacher/master expressions common today, for they imply a control and dependency that can only produce a spiritual pathology–on both sides. How rare is a friend of the soul that will teach the needful–and no more. It is only the incompetent teacher that keeps the student enthralled in a personality cult that substitutes for the spiritual development and experience the teacher's instructions cannot lead to. My beloved friend Swami Sivananda of Rishikesh would advise a disciple to live with him only a few months and then go and attain something for himself and not turn Sivananda into some kind of private deity to be adored and served to the neglect of the disciple's progress. Swami Ramdas of Anandashram was also insistent about this. In the May, 2002 issue of *The Vision*, the Anandashram magazine, the following words from one of his letters appeared on page 294: "You cannot deny the fact that those who attached themselves to the person of a guru did not rise up to the guru's stature. The spiritual heroes are those who, through the contact of a saint, get inner awakening and by standing alone develop divine perfection. ...whereas, a long, continued company of the guru is far from helpful and elevating. This has been Ramdas' experience since our Ashram came into existence. The pearl oyster receives the drop and dives down to fashion it into a beautiful pearl by its own tapasya as it were." Earlier in the issue he states that real service to the guru is doing spiritual practice and attaining enlightenment—not flattering the guru and running enterprises and projects in his name. Such honest teachers are rare, alas. Right now I know of only one, and his disciples are continually griping because he refuses to run their lives and dot all their i's and cross all their t's for them. They have no idea what a treasure they have, perhaps because they do not really want what he has to give: the path to liberation.

Blind

"And he spake a parable unto them, Can the blind lead the blind? shall they not both fall into the ditch?" (Luke 6:39). The idea is clear. So also is the statement of Saint Paul that "as many as are led by the Spirit of God, they are the sons of God" (Romans 8:14). And before that Isaiah: "I am the Lord thy God, which leadeth thee by the way that thou shouldest go" (Isaiah 48:17). The internal guide—our own spirit in communion with the Supreme Spirit—can and will do the needful. Looking outward for lifetimes we have only become increasingly enmeshed in ignorance. Only when we look within will we find "the way, the truth, and the life" (John 14:6). Remember the dictum of the teacher in the Chandogya Upanishad: "Thou art That" and act accordingly after finding your true "thou" through meditation and spiritual discipline.

If those who lead you say to you, "See, the kingdom is in the sky," then the birds of the sky will precede you. If they say to you, "It is in the sea," then the fish will precede you. The poet-saint Mirabai expressed this idea in one of her songs quoted by Yogananda in the seventh chapter of *Autobiography of a Yogi:*

If by bathing daily God could be realized
Sooner would I be a whale in the deep;
If by eating roots and fruits He could be known
Gladly would I choose the form of a goat;
If the counting of rosaries uncovered Him
I would say my prayers on mammoth beads;
If bowing before stone images unveiled Him
A flinty mountain I would humbly worship;
If by drinking milk the Lord could be imbibed
Many calves and children would know Him.

The error of all these views cited by Jesus and Mirabai is that God is far away–far from us in some inaccessible hidden depths. Such a view suits opportunistic religionists very well, because it necessitates a chain of intermediaries upon whom the aspirant must be forever wholly dependent.

Rather, the kingdom is inside of you, and it is outside of you. The divine kingdom is right at hand, not far away and unreachable or accessible only through terrible struggles. Yet, we do not see the kingdom, much less dwell within it on a conscious level. What must be done to perceive the kingdom?

When you come to know yourselves, then you will become known. Self-knowledge is essential and imperative. These words of Jesus are a distillation of a part of the Chandogya Upanishad which was surely well-known to him. Though a bit long, I am inserting it here in the excellent version by Swami Prabhavananda in *The Upanishads, Breath of the Eternal:*

When Svetaketu was twelve years old, his father Uddalaka said to him, "Svetaketu, you must now go to school and study. None of our family, my child, is ignorant of Brahman."

Thereupon Svetaketu went to a teacher and studied for twelve years. After committing to memory all the Vedas, he returned home full of pride in his learning.

His father, noticing the young man's conceit, said to him: "Svetaketu, have you asked for that knowledge by which we hear the unbearable, by which we perceive the unperceivable, by which we know the unknowable?"

"What is that knowledge, sir?" asked Svetaketu.

"My child, as by knowing one lump of clay, all things made of clay are known, the difference being only in name and arising from speech, and the truth being that all are clay; as by knowing a nugget of gold, all things made of gold are known, the difference being only in name and arising from speech, and the truth being that all are gold–exactly so is that knowledge, knowing which we know all."

"But surely those venerable teachers of mine are ignorant of this knowledge; for if they had possessed it, they would have taught it to me. Do you therefore, sir, give me that knowledge."

"Be it so," said Uddalaka, and continued thus:

"In the beginning there was Existence, One only, without a second. Some say that in the beginning there was nonexistence only, and that out of that the universe was born. But how could such a thing be? How could existence be born of non-existence? No, my son, in the beginning there was Existence alone–One only, without a second. He, the One, thought to himself: Let me be many, let me grow forth. Thus out of himself he projected the universe; and having projected out of himself the universe, he entered into every being. All that is has its self in him alone. Of all things he is the subtle essence. He is the truth. He is the Self. And that, Svetaketu, THAT ART THOU."

"Please, sir, tell me more about this Self."

"Be it so, my child:

"As the bees make honey by gathering juices from many flowering plants and trees, and as these juices reduced to one honey do not know from what flowers they severally come, similarly, my son, all creatures, when they are merged in that one Existence, whether in dreamless sleep or in death, know nothing of their past or present state, because of the ignorance enveloping them–know not that they are merged in him and that from him they came.

"Whatever these creatures are, whether a lion, or a tiger, or a boar, or a worm, or a gnat, or a mosquito, that they remain after they come back from dreamless sleep.

"All these have their self in him alone. He is the truth. He is the subtle essence of all. He is the Self. And that, Svetaketu, THAT ART THOU."

"Please, sir, tell me more about this Self."

"Be it so, my son:

"The rivers in the east flow eastward, the rivers in the west flow westward, and all enter into the sea. From sea to sea they pass, the clouds lifting them to the sky as vapor and sending them down as rain. And as these rivers, when they are united with the sea, do not know whether they are this or that river, likewise all those creatures that I have named, when they have come back from Brahman, know not whence they came.

"All those beings have their self in him alone. He is the truth. He is the subtle essence of all. He is the Self. And that, Svetaketu, THAT ART THOU."

"Please, sir, tell me more about this Self."

"Be it so, my child:

"If someone were to strike once at the root of this large tree, it would bleed, but live. If he were to strike at its stem, it would bleed, but live. If he were to strike at the top, it would bleed, but live. Pervaded by the living Self, this tree stands firm, and takes its food; but if the Self were to depart from one of its branches, that branch would wither; if it were to depart from a second, that would wither; if it were to depart from a third, that would wither. If it were to depart from the whole tree, the whole tree would wither.

"Likewise, my son, know this: The body dies when the Self leaves it–but the Self dies not.

"All that is has its self in him alone. He is the truth. He is the subtle essence of all. He is the Self. And that, Svetaketu, THAT ART THOU."

"Please, sir, tell me more about this Self."

"Be it so. Bring a fruit of that Nyagrodha tree."

"Here it is, sir."

"Break it."

"It is broken, sir."

"What do you see?"

"Some seeds, extremely small, sir."

"Break one of them."

"It is broken, sir."

"What do you see?"

"Nothing, sir."

"The subtle essence you do not see, and in that is the whole of the Nyagrodha tree. Believe, my son, that that which is the subtle essence–in that have all things their existence. That is the truth. That is the Self. And that, Svetaketu, THAT ART THOU."

"Please, sir, tell me more about this Self."

"Be it so. Put this salt in water, and come to me tomorrow morning."

Svetaketu did as he was bidden. The next morning his father asked him to bring the salt which he had put in the water. But he could not, for it had dissolved. Then said Uddalaka:

"Sip the water, and tell me how it tastes."

"It is salty, sir."

"In the same way," continued Uddalaka, "though you do not see Brahman in this body, he is indeed here. That which is the subtle essence–in that have all things their existence. That is the truth. That is the Self. And that, Svetaketu, THAT ART THOU."

"Please, sir, tell me more about this Self," said the youth again.

"Be it so, my child:

"As a man may be blindfolded, and led away, and left in a strange place; and as, having been so dealt with, he turns in every direction and cries out for someone to remove his bandages and show him the way home; and as one thus entreated may loose his bandages and give him comfort; and as thereupon he walks from village to village, asking his way as he goes; and as he arrives home at last—just so does a man who meets with an illumined teacher obtain true knowledge.

"That which is the subtle essence—in that have all beings their existence. That is the truth. That is the Self. And that, O Svetaketu, THAT ART THOU."

"Please, sir, tell me more about this Self."

"Be it so, my child:

"When a man is fatally ill, his relations gather round him and ask, 'Do you know me? Do you know me?' Now until his speech is merged in his mind, his mind in his breath, his breath in his vital heat, his vital heat in the Supreme Being, he knows them. But when his speech is merged in his mind, his mind in his breath, his breath in his vital heat, his vital heat in the Supreme Being, then he does not know them.

"That which is the subtle essence—in that have all beings their existence. That is the truth. That is the Self. And that, O Svetaketu, THAT ART THOU."

What more could possibly be said about self-knowledge?

There is one point of interest. Jesus says that when we come to know ourselves we will become known ourselves. Saint Paul wrote a little more fully of this, saying: "For now we see through a glass, darkly; but then face to face: now I know in part; *but then shall I know even as also I am known*" (I Corinthians 13:12).

And you will realize that it is you who are the sons of the living father. The idea is that of conscious communication with God: God knowing us fully and us knowing Him fully. It is a matter of *identity*, of our oneness with God and His oneness with us.

But if you will not know yourselves, you dwell in poverty. In Revelation Jesus speaks to us all, saying: "Thou sayest, I am rich, and increased with goods, and have need of nothing; and knowest not that thou art wretched, and miserable, and poor, and blind, and naked" (Revelation

3:17). This is the plight of those who know not themselves, to whom Jesus makes the stern indictment:

And it is you who are that poverty. Those without self-realization are poverty itself.

"The kingdom of heaven is like unto treasure hid in a field; the which when a man hath found, he hideth, and for joy thereof goeth and selleth all that he hath, and buyeth that field" (Matthew 13:44). The wise seek the inner treasure that makes all men more than rich.

THE ONE GOAL

Jesus said, The man old in days will not hesitate to ask a small child seven days old about the place of life, and he will live. For many who are first will become last, and they will become one and the same. (4)

The man old in days will not hesitate to ask a small child seven days old about the place of life, and he will live. This is a prime example of a metaphysical statement that can be taken in more than one way–all of them wise. Whether this multiple-level meaning is intentional or whether commentators are simply ingenious in reading unintended subtleties into the sacred words is really undeterminable. In the study of scriptures there are two equally unfortunate pitfalls: 1) failing to see the meaning, and 2) seeing meaning where none was intended. The following story from *Zen Flesh, Zen Bones*, illustrates this very well.

"Provided he makes and wins an argument about Buddhism with those who live there, any wandering monk can remain in a Zen temple. If he is defeated, he has to move on.

"In a temple in the northern part of Japan two brother monks were dwelling together. The elder one was learned, but the younger one was stupid and had but one eye.

"A wandering monk came and asked for lodging, properly challenging them to a debate about the sublime teaching. The elder brother, tired that day from much studying, told the younger one to take his place. 'Go and request the dialogue in silence,' he cautioned.

"So the young monk and the stranger went to the shrine and sat down.

"Shortly afterwards the traveler rose and went in to the elder brother and said: 'Your young brother is a wonderful fellow. He defeated me.'

"'Relate the dialogue to me,' said the elder one.

"'Well,' explained the traveler, 'first I held up one finger, representing Buddha, the enlightened one. So he held up two fingers, signifying Buddha and his teaching. I held up three fingers, representing Buddha, his teaching, and his followers, living the harmonious life. Then he shook his clenched fist in my face, indicating that all three come from one realization. Thus he won and so I have no right to remain here.' With this, the traveller left.

"'Where is that fellow?' asked the younger one, running in to his elder brother.

"'I understand you won the debate.'

"'Won, nothing. I'm going to beat him up.'

"'Tell me the subject of the debate,' asked the elder one.

"'Why, the minute he saw me he held up one finger, insulting me by insinuating that I have only one eye. Since he was a stranger I thought I would be polite to him, so I held up two fingers, congratulating him that he has two eyes. Then the impolite wretch help up three fingers, suggesting that between us we only have three eyes. So I got mad and started to punch him, but he ran out and that ended it!'"

Reading wisdom into inane or foolish words is a particular skill of the East, as is making ingenious (and ingenuous) rationalization for nonsensical and even evil deeds committed by spiritual figures–taking folly and evil and making them seem wisdom and virtue. Writing about Eastern texts in the context of Eastern thought, a commentator must assiduously avoid this pitfall, although few do. And his readers should be equally cautious about accepting any interpretations without careful consideration and thought. Discrimination is always wisdom, though the sentimentalism current in most religion runs counter to it. Now having said that I will warily try to comment on this fourth verse of the Gospel of Thomas.

Metaphysical age

Most spiritual traditions use age references to indicate spiritual levels. Even in cultures where age is respected and people are proud of their advanced years, "old" means mired in time, "aged" by identification with external existence, marked by the conditionings of many lives. "Young," on the other hand, means one who has become rejuvenated in the spirit by erasure of those metaphysical "age wrinkles" and regained his original spiritual vigor. Such a person is not a blank as he was at the beginning of his peregrinations through many rebirths, but retains all the growth he has attained while "young" in spiritual vigor and refreshment. In the New Testament we read a goodly bit about "old" versus "new" men: "Knowing this, that our old man is crucified with him, that the body of sin might be destroyed, that henceforth we should not serve sin" (Romans 6:6). "That ye put off concerning the former conversation the old man, which is corrupt according to the deceitful lusts; and be renewed in the spirit of your mind; and that ye put on the new man, which after God is created in righteousness and true holiness" (Ephesians 4:22-24). "Lie not one to another, seeing that ye have put off the old man with his deeds; and have put on the new man, which is renewed in knowledge after the image of him that created him" (Colossians 3:9,10).

We are also told about the renewal of consciousness in becoming "as a child" in the spirit. "Jesus called a little child unto him, and set him in the midst of them, and said, Verily I say unto you, Except ye be converted, and become as little children, ye shall not enter into the kingdom of heaven. Whosoever therefore shall humble himself as this little child, the same is greatest in the kingdom of heaven" (Matthew

18:2-4). We are told that "children" are the natural inhabitants of the Kingdom of God Consciousness. "Then were there brought unto him little children, that he should put his hands on them, and pray: and the disciples rebuked them. But Jesus said, Suffer little children, and forbid them not, to come unto me: for of such is the kingdom of heaven" (Matthew 19:13,14).

Saint Paul writes about the "days" of evolution and their number, harking back to the "days" of Genesis that symbolize the stages of unfolding consciousness. (See the fourth chapter of Hebrews and the first chapters of Genesis.) A "man old in days" is someone that is worn and weary from the troubles and uncertainties of many births. "A small child seven days old" is one who has traversed the seven levels of spiritual development and renewed himself within. Such a "young" one should be approached by the "old" even if their chronological ages are reversed.

I saw this very clearly during my first trip to India. More than once I saw adults taking very seriously the words of children in relation to spiritual matters. In one ashram I attended a gathering of adults to listen to a small boy recount his meditation experiences and what he had concluded from them. After some discussion they unanimously told the boy they were confident that his experiences were real and that he should act on them. "A little child shall lead them" (Isaiah 11:6) is accepted in India, though hardly ever in the supposedly Christian West.

In his Hymn to Dakshinamurti [Shiva], Shankara writes of the aged disciples surrounding the youthful guru. It is often seen that externally aged teachers show more youth than their seemingly younger students. It is all in the heart.

The place of life

The "old" will ask the "young" about "the place of life." The place of life is where the Lifegiver is to be found, and that is the heart of each seeker. "I am the Self abiding in the heart of all beings; I am the beginning, the middle and the end of all beings as well" (Bhagavad Gita

10:20). "With hands and feet everywhere, eyes, heads and faces everywhere, with ears throughout the universe–THAT stands, enveloping everything. Having the appearance of all the qualities of the senses, yet free of all the senses, unattached yet maintaining all, free from the gunas, yet experiencing the gunas, outside and inside beings–the animate and the inanimate–incomprehensible because of its subtlety, far away and also near, undivided, yet remaining as if divided in beings, this is to be known as the sustainer of beings, their absorber and generator. Also this is said to be the light of lights, beyond all darkness; knowledge, the to-be-known, the goal of knowledge seated in the heart of all" (Bhagavad Gita 13:13-17).

Those who seek within and find that place of life and the Lifegiver himself shall truly live, for: "The Lord lives in the heart of every creature. He turns them round and round upon the wheel of his Maya. Take refuge utterly in him. By his grace you will find supreme peace, and the state which is beyond all change" (Bhagavad Gita 18:61-62).

For many who are first will become last, and they will become one and the same. The first half of this sentence is expounded in the Gospel of Matthew: "Many that are first shall be last; and the last shall be first. For the kingdom of heaven is like unto a man that is an householder, which went out early in the morning to hire labourers into his vineyard. And when he had agreed with the labourers for a penny a day, he sent them into his vineyard. And he went out about the third hour, and saw others standing idle in the marketplace, And said unto them; Go ye also into the vineyard, and whatsoever is right I will give you. And they went their way. Again he went out about the sixth and ninth hour, and did likewise. And about the eleventh hour he went out, and found others standing idle, and saith unto them, Why stand ye here all the day idle? They say unto him, Because no man hath hired us. He saith unto them, Go ye also into the vineyard; and whatsoever is right, that shall ye receive. So when even was come, the lord of the vineyard saith unto his steward, Call the labourers, and give them their hire, beginning from the last unto the first. And when they came that were hired about the eleventh hour, they received every man a penny. But when the first came, they supposed that they should have received more; and they likewise received every man a penny. And when they had received it, they murmured against the goodman of the house, saying, These last have wrought but one hour, and thou hast made them equal unto us, which have borne the burden and heat of the day. But he answered one of them, and said, Friend, I do thee no wrong: didst not thou agree with me for a penny? Take that thine is, and go thy way: I will give unto this last, even as unto thee. Is it not lawful for me to do what I will with mine own? Is thine eye evil, because I am good? So the last shall be first, and the first last: for many be called, but few chosen" (Matthew 19:30; 20:1-16).

The idea behind all this is that the goal is absolutely the same, and the attainment for each one of us is identical, whether we reach it early or late. It is often supposed that some people attain liberation very easily in a short time, but this does not take into account what may be hundreds of previous lives of spiritual effort. Conversely, someone who may seek for an entire lifetime before attaining any perceivable result may only have a comparatively few lifetimes of effort behind him. But at the end all are the same, for all spirits are identical in scope of consciousness. In the kingdom of heaven there are no greater and lesser citizens, only divine rays of the Divine Light.

Becoming "one and the same" implies more than equality of rank. It means that everyone will have perfect realization and unity with both one another and with God—that every drop in the ocean of light shall be united and share in one another's being as much as they share in God's infinite Being. "And so shall we ever be with the Lord" (I Thessalonians 4:17) and each other.

FROM THE SEEN TO THE UNSEEN

Jesus said, Recognize what is in your sight, and that which is hidden from you will become plain to you. For there is nothing hidden which will not become manifest. (5. *See Matthew 10:26, Mark 4:22, Luke 8:17, and Luke 12:2*)

I f we do not comprehend our real nature, who/what we really are, then we can understand nothing about our life. But it is equally necessary to have an understanding of the nature of the world around us. Dualistic philosophy postulates that we are spirits, whereas the world is matter only, that we are imprisoned in the world, and to escape from it somehow is liberation of the spirit. A misunderstanding of yoga seems to reinforce this, and most yogis subscribe to a dualistic view of things, though it may be overlaid with a veneer of non-dualism. Certainly the world is a prison, but only because we have imprisoned ourselves. A door can either keep us in or let us out—it depends on how we use it. We are the wardens of our own prison.

What is the purpose of the world? If we see it as a morass into which we have fallen and become entangled we will respond to it accordingly.

If, however, we realize that the world is an instrument for our evolution, that it is itself an essential part of our liberation, we will think of it much differently than do most "spiritual" people, and we will approach and utilize it in that different perspective.

My beloved friend, Swami Sivananda of Rishikesh, wrote a poem entitled "Only God I Saw" in which he described seeing the entire world and all within it as a manifestation of Divinity. If we can really "see" with the awakened eye of our spirit that the entire field of relative existence is Divine, in that very moment we will see "that which is hidden." The seeing and the revealing are simultaneous. Nothing remains unseen to the awakened sight. Nothing. One translation says: "Recognize Him in front of your face…." This brings to mind the opening verse of the Isha Upanishad: "All this–whatever exists in this changing universe–should be covered by the Lord."

To recap: We are not to turn from the world; if we do that we will never see truly. Rather, we are to open the inner eye, remove what Shankara called "the glaucoma of ignorance," and find ourselves face to face with Spirit. Those who seek spirit by shunning the world, longing for "blessed death" and such, will fulfill the declaration of the Isha Upanishad's ninth verse that those who reject relative existence enter into an even greater darkness than those who plunge into materiality, denying or ignoring the existence of the spirit. For, disengaging themselves from the world, they will never solve its riddle and be free.

WHAT JESUS WANTS US TO DO

His disciples questioned him and said to him, Do you want us to fast? How shall we pray? Shall we give alms? What diet shall we observe? Jesus said, Do not tell lies, and do not do what you hate, for all things are plain in the sight of heaven. For nothing hidden will not become manifest, and nothing covered will remain without being uncovered. (6)

"What would Jesus do?" has become a faddish saying in the past few years, although the books *In His Steps* and *What Would Jesus Do?* were written over a hundred years ago. Actually the question is irrelevant, because neither you nor I are Jesus. The relevant question is: What should *I* do? For as Krishna says in the Bhagavad Gita: "Better is one's swadharma, though deficient, than the swadharma of another well performed. Better is death in one's own swadharma. The swadharma of another brings danger (Bhagavad Gita 3:35).

His disciples questioned him and said to him, "Do you want us to fast? How shall we pray? Shall we give alms? What diet shall we observe?" The disciples of Jesus apparently had an opinion regarding what was incumbent

28

on all seekers of truth, and therefore asked the foregoing. As was so often the case with Jesus, he refused to go along with the matters set before him by others and insisted on telling them what the real questions were. And then he gave them the answers.

Here we see that the disciples were interested in fasting, praying, alms-giving, and dietary discipline–all of which have value and are enjoined by all viable religious traditions. But of themselves they mean very little. The disciples had not yet understood the basics, the foundation without which any superstructure would be doomed to collapse.

Do not tell lies. There are many ways to lie: by words, by silence, and by actions. What Jesus is telling the disciples is Live Truthfully, that is: live the truth, be embodiments of the truth. And what is the truth? God. So Jesus is telling the disciples to live God–to manifest the divinity that is inherent in them and in all beings. Later Saint Paul would write about the necessity to be numbered among those "who walk not after the flesh, but after the Spirit. For… ye are not in the flesh, but in the Spirit" (Romans 8:4-6, 9). It is not a matter of being "bad" or "good" but of being truthful. To live as a material being is to live a lie; to live as a spiritual being is to live the truth. And that is truly "life and peace." "This I say then, Walk in the Spirit," for "he that is joined unto the Lord is one spirit" with the Divine (Galatians 5:16; I Corinthians 6:17).

Do not do what you hate. Hypocrisy is also a form of lying in life, therefore Jesus tells the disciples to not do what they hate–what they have an aversion to. He is not speaking of indulging the childish, egoic whim that functions solely on the level of "I like it" or "I don't like it," but rather of the developing spiritual and intuitive sense of right and wrong–the conscience of the spirit.

No outer authority should determine our actions. We alone must live our life. Does that mean we should not listen to holy books or spiritual teachers? No, but it does mean that our own inner certainty must deter-mine whether or not we follow the counsels of those "authorities." There are mindless slaves who do whatever they are told and quote scriptures and teachers like parrots to justify their zombie existence. But those with awakened consciousness realize that ultimately it is their decision as to whether they follow external advice or not. "God says to do it, so I shall," is actually a statement of personal will—at least when made rightly. When Jesus said: "Not my will, but thine, be done" (Luke 22:42), he was making a supreme act of will.

There is no place here for "surrender" or suchlike, though it is a favorite in cult religion. God is not our enemy, God is our essential Being. Wherefore Krishna says: "I am the same to all beings. There is no one who is disliked or dear to me. But they who worship me with devotion are in me, and I am also in them" (Bhagavad Gita 9:29).

For all things are plain in the sight of heaven. For nothing hidden will not become manifest, and nothing covered will remain without being uncovered. There are two "heavens," one outer and one inner. The outer heaven is the infinite expanse of Divine Being, and the inner heaven is the highest level of our own individual being, where the finite and the Infinite touch and are one. Neither of them can be fooled by our egos. At the beginning of the film *Almost An Angel* the main character is in the hospital and has what seems to be an out of the body experience. He meets God (played by Charlton Heston) and comments on how much He looks like Charlton Heston. Then he says: "You're God; I can't lie to You, can I?" To which God dryly replies: "You can try."

The wise do not try.

EAT OR BE EATEN

Jesus said, Blessed is the lion which becomes man when consumed by man; and cursed is the man whom the lion consumes, and the lion becomes man. (7)

The lion-faced power

It would be impossible to figure out the meaning of this by mere reasoning, however symbolical we might try to be. We must understand the historical situation in the Mediterranean world at the time these words were spoken. More than one school of esoteric thought spoke of "the lion-faced power." Some schools meant the negative power within the cosmos, also called Satan. Saint Peter had this in mind when he wrote: "Be sober, be vigilant; because your adversary the devil, as a roaring lion, walketh about, seeking whom he may devour: Whom resist steadfast in the faith" (I Peter 5:8, 9). Others meant the raw power of the cosmos with which we can do as we will, as long as we can control (master) it–for if we cannot, it will overcome us instead of us overcoming it. Others considered the lion-faced power to be both the raw material of the universe and at the same time an intelligent Providence which reacted according to the motivation or purpose of those who would tap it. That is, those whose intention was negative or foolish would be reacted to in a way that might appear to be punishment or retribution, but was really only a mirroring of their inner mind and outer deeds. If they were destructive then they would be destroyed; if harmful they would be harmed; if beneficial they would be benefited; if divine they would be divinized. Those who approached matter in the consciousness or perspective of spirit would find the world to be spirit. Those who treated it as dead or unconscious would themselves become dead–unconscious. So to approach the power was hazardous for the ignorant or the ill-intentioned.

There is no such thing as a pure object. That is, everything within the cosmos is within us, is subjective to a very real degree. Whatever we do to an external object occurs to its counterpart within us–occurs to us. In a way that has already been outlined above, but it is good to express it in a different way so we get the idea: nothing is trivial; we must approach life and the world within which we live with utter seriousness of intention.

Whenever we interact, even mentally, with the world, we devour it in the sense that we assimilate it through the reaction that takes place inwardly. Just as we assimilate and utilize the food we eat, so it is with any contact we have with the world–and especially if we tap into the deeper levels of existence.

Christian perspective

Christians also were aware of the lion-faced power and its dilemma for the actively questing soul, as the text known as the *Pistis Sophia* shows. A very much later indication of this awareness is to be found, interestingly enough, in the tarot deck designed by A. E. Waite, the English nineteenth/twentieth century Christian esotericist.

Perhaps the most common and perilous approach to the lion-faced power is the contracting of relationships. For then we are integrating with another living reflection of the cosmos in all its complexity and perplexity. Superficial, sex-oriented people think that the favoring of monastic life within a spiritual tradition is based on a rejection of sex, when in actuality it is the solitariness of the untouched and untouching celibate monastic life that is the real secret of its spiritual power and safety. The same is true of the dedicated yogi. "The yogi should fix his awareness constantly on the Self, remaining in solitude" (Bhagavad Gita 6:10). "[Have] unswerving devotion to me with single-minded yoga, living in secluded places, having distaste for association with many people" (Bhagavad Gita 13:10). "Dwelling in a solitary place,... he is fit for union with Brahman" (Bhagavad Gita 18:52-53). Knowing this, the celibate Waite designed the card known as The Two of Cups accordingly. He directed the artist Pamela Coleman Smith to show a man and woman standing facing one another and exchanging cups. The scene is very tranquil and shows both depth and delicacy of feeling–both rare in most instances, and therefore all the more relevant to those evolved enough to be seeking understanding of human life so as to aspire to divine life.

But there is something else in the picture. Right between the two cups is seen a caduceus, the staff of Aescalepius, the healer of the gods, with its two intertwined serpents symbolizing the inner power of both the lovers as well as the positive and negative force inherent in all things, deeds, and thoughts. Above the caduceus, borne aloft on powerful wings, broods the face of a lion, a face both powerful and ominous, even threatening. However tranquil the picture may be, it reveals tremendous risk and danger. It is the character and intent of the two cupbearers that will determine the reaction of this overshadowing Presence. And this is true of us in all situations. None of us can legitimately say: "It is my life; I will do with it what I want." It is not our life at all. It is only borrowed from the power, and we must live accordingly every moment.

Blessing or cursing

So now, with this as background let us look at the words of Jesus: "Blessed is the lion which becomes man when consumed by man; and cursed is the man whom the lion consumes, and the lion becomes man."

The sole purpose of the creation is the liberation of the individual spirits within it. Even though we may smile with genteel contempt at the earlier idea that the sun goes around the earth, which is the center of the entire cosmos, and that everything upon the earth is for either the domination or the enjoyment of human beings, the bedrock truth is this: the entire range of relative existence, including this planet, has been manifested for the liberation of the evolving spirit. Of course, that includes every single atom, each of which is a potential divinity. Human beings are but a part of creation's intent. The Sufi poet, Rumi, wrote:

> A stone I died and rose again a plant.
> A plant I died and rose an animal;
> I died an animal and was born a man.
> Why should I fear? What have I lost by death?
> As man, death sweeps me from this world of men
> That I may wear an angel's wings in heaven;
> Yet e'en as angel may I not abide,
> For nought abideth save the face of God.
> Thus o'er the angels' world I wing my way
> Onwards and upwards, unto boundless lights;
> Then let me be as nought, for in my heart
> Rings as a harp-song that we must return to Him.

Oliver Wendell Holmes, one of many great Americans whose belief in reincarnation is overlooked, wrote in his poem, *The Chambered Nautilus:*

> Build thee more stately mansions, O my soul!
> As the swift seasons roll!
> Leave thy low-vaulted past!
> Let each new temple, nobler than the last,
> Shut thee from heaven with a dome more vast,

Till thou at length art free,
Leaving thine outgrown shell by life's unresting sea!

Eat or be eaten

It is true: relativity either eats us or we eat it. We consume it or are consumed by it. The first is growth and eventual liberation, the second is a sliding backwards and increased bondage.

There are three processes of the spirit-intelligence in relation to relative existence: involution, evolution, and devolution. First we enter fully into relative existence and take on a vehicle for function therein. This is involution. Hopefully we so function as to develop our awareness and move onward into increasingly complex body-vehicles which increasingly express our consciousness-nature. This is evolution. If we malfunction within creation, we stagnate and regress. This is devolution. Those who "eat" the lion master it (or at least the part of it that they are working on at the time) and make it part of their expanding manifestation. Those who are "eaten" by the lion are lessened or contracted by it and expelled back down the path of evolution. It thus increases (regains) its mastery-dominance to some degree and is "blessed" while the devolved soul is "cursed" by its very situation.

From this we can see that it is the lion-faced power which we mistake for both God and the Devil (Satan). Both experiences are illusions, Divinity being completely beyond that power. And yet it is a manifestation of Deity. It will take a great deal more evolution on our part before we comprehend this fully. Until then we must keep on "eating" and nevermore be "eaten."

FISHING WISELY

And he said, The man is like a wise fisherman who cast his net into the sea and drew it up from the sea full of small fish. Among them the wise fisherman found a fine large fish. He threw all the small fish back into the sea and chose the large fish without difficulty. Whoever has ears to hear, let him hear. (8)

The man

By just saying "the man" Jesus is being very oriental, for in the East it is considered an absolute that no one is really a human being until he has attained the state of consciousness that befits the human level of evolution. That is why in some texts there is insistence that all human beings, or everyone or the whole world. engages in praise and worship of God. Those who do not are simply not human in the evolutionary sense, though they are certainly moving toward that point, and not to be despised or discounted.

In the Gospel of Matthew Jesus is quoted as saying "the kingdom of heaven" rather than "the man," but when we consider it, a human being is a kingdom of heaven, albeit an unrealized and unmanifested heaven.

The wise fisherman

A wise fisherman is someone who casts the net of his consciousness into the sea of the cosmos and correctly evaluates whatever he draws up into it. Being wise, he seeks for "that one thing, which when known, all else is known" (Mundaka Upanishad 1.1.3). To get to that he must not be satisfied with anything less than the One. This is extremely difficult, for to our presently small minds so many things appear to be tremendous, yet they are really very small. Since they fill the scope of our limited awareness we may think they are infinite, but they are nothing in comparison to the Real which we seek. This is the great pitfall of many yogis. It is so easy to settle for so much less than is our destiny, to become satisfied with only the shadow of that which we seek. We, too, like a wise fisherman, have to keep tossing the small fry back into the sea until only the big fish of Divine Consciousness remains.

Sri Ramakrishna spoke of how in a deep pool there sometimes would be found one huge fish, a legendary fish that so many anglers tried to hook. But, being old and clever, the fish would elude the hook but get the bait. The fish, he said, was like Brahman itself: elusive, but worth the patient wait and the development of the skill needed to draw it to us.

Give heed

"Whoever has ears to hear, let him hear," because only those who toss the small fish back into the sea really choose the large fish we are after. Many try to hold on to both, but end up with only the small things. We must hold to the One to the exclusion of all else. It is really easy to do ("without difficulty") if we let go of all the fish, not keeping hold of the tiniest minnow or even a fish egg! Those who find it hard are holding on to something other than the One.

THE INNER FIELD

Jesus said, Now the sower went out, took a handful (of seeds), and scattered them. Some fell on the road; the birds came and gathered them up. Others fell on the rock, did not take root in the soil, and did not produce ears. And others fell on thorns; they choked the seed(s) and worms ate them. And others fell on the good soil and it produced good fruit: it bore sixty per measure and a hundred and twenty per measure. (9)

Now the sower went out, took a handful (of seeds), and scattered them. This is a picture of wisdom entering into the life spheres of various individuals, and is also a portrayal of the individual cultivating higher consciousness under his own will. It is a consideration of spiritual environment. Krishna says in the Bhagavad Gita: "This body is called the Field, and he who knows this is called the Knower of the Field–so say the knowers of these things" (Bhagavad Gita 13:1).

The world is said to be the body or vehicle of God, just as our bodies are the vehicles of our spirits. Both we and God are engaging in the process of evolution–not of our spirit being, for that is eternally perfect, but of our body-instruments so they may reveal and manifest the light of Spirit.

Perhaps the most important point in this quotation is the fact that Jesus is speaking only of the environment of the seeds–not the seeds themselves, for they are without defect, perfect. In this way Jesus is telling us what kind of inner and outer environment we must create for our spiritual progress. Our inner perfection means nothing if we cannot manifest it, for that is the sole purpose of our being here in the world and undergoing the process we call life.

Some fell on the road; the birds came and gathered them up. The constant traffic moved them around and prevented their taking root. Busyness is perhaps the worst possible environment for spiritual progress. Activity is necessary for any growth, but busyness is constant involvement with external factors and short-term goals. It is the trivializing of the human being, however much others may admire the busy person. Some people are always on the go to cover up the void and discontent that would impinge on their awareness if they allowed themselves to become still for even a moment. Others are chronic worriers and busybodies because it amuses them and occupies their idle minds. In contrast there are those whose professions or situation in life demand continual dedication to outer action. If it would be suggested to them that they should change professions or situations they would be indignant, insisting that their activities are indicative of their being responsible and conscientious regarding their duties, that to do otherwise would be to be selfish or slackers. Running in their self-satisfied hamster wheels they will never get anywhere, because the birds of constant anxiety and outer demands preclude any possible interior growth. They are so busy "serving humanity" they have no time to fullfil the sole purpose of humanity. They think the world could not manage without them. But as DeGaulle remarked, the cemeteries of the world are filled with "indispensable" people. Any of these people could stop the traffic and shoo away the birds at any moment if they wanted to.

Others fell on the rock, did not take root in the soil, and did not produce ears. The road was soil (remember, Jesus is speaking at a time when all roads were dirt tracks except for some of the Roman roads that were paved with stone) and at least had a potential for growth. But there are environments, internal and external, that simply give no possibility of sprouting. They are the rocks. In early Christian documents we find lists of professions or situations in life which prevented someone from becoming a Christian. These lists were not based on the idea that those professions or situations were sinful, but rather on the fact that they rendered those involved in them *incapable* of spiritual life. Such situations do exist. I do not see any need to list them, because it would be impossible to make a complete list, and a little thought with good sense reveals what they are. It is only wisdom for us to continually evaluate our inner and outer situations and ask the question: Is this conducive to spiritual life or does it contradict or stagnate spiritual life?

When I was eighteen and searching fervently for truth, I attended a church meeting in the summer. One of the ministers was a most unusual man with great experience in the spiritual quest. On the final day of the meeting he asked to speak with me. We went and sat in the main auditorium. Without preamble he opened his Bible and read: "He that dwelleth in the secret place of the most High shall abide under the shadow of the Almighty" (Psalms 91:1). Then he spoke briefly about the necessity for me to always check my situation to make sure I was really "under the shadow of the Almighty." His counsel was prophetic, because I went from there to another state where I got a position in the office of what we then called "a radio preacher." This man was heard throughout the United States and even in some foreign countries. But he was a crook on all levels. After a few days I sat at my desk and asked myself straightforwardly if I was "under the shadow of the Almighty" working in such a place. Of course I was not. So, although it was a very high-paying job, I quit.

Ray Bradbury gave a talk at a university writing class in which he told the students that if anything in their life–including some person–was blocking their becoming writers they should get rid of it immediately.

He further said that aspiring writers should get divorces if need be. Everybody chuckled and thought that was cute. But what if he had enunciated that principle in relation to spiritual life? He would have been branded a fanatic. Nonetheless it is true that we must ruthlessly reorder our life if its present status hinders or prevents spiritual life. As Swami Trigunatitananda used to say: "Do or die–but you won't die!"

Others fell on thorns; they choked the seed(s) and worms ate them. Some environments are too agitated (busy), some are simply impossible for growth, and then there are those in which the elements of the environment completely overshadow and distract the seeker from the quest. These are the "thorns." Sometimes they are distracting by their inherent nature, and sometimes the seeker is too susceptible to their influence or effect. But however it may be, the quest becomes crowded out of the mind and heart, and the "worms" of distraction and attraction annihilate the upward impulse and end the journey for that life. In how many lives has the same happened to us?

"Thorns" take many forms, some pleasant and some painful. It seems a necessary part of each one's story that temptations must arise to reveal the depth and quality of our aspiration. Infinite is the number and variety of the thorns that snag human beings and stop them on their upward striving. This is especially true of those that have turned to spiritual life more from frustration and disappointment than from a real desire to know God. Inevitably it happens that some greatly desired object is–at least seemingly–offered to them. But to have the desired thing, spiritual life must be laid aside–and it usually is. Sometimes the distracted aspirant really gets what he wants, but usually he never gets it or it is taken from him after a short while and he ends up with nothing. Tragically, such a one never turns back to the search for higher life, but passes his life in desolation, almost unaware of what has happened to him.

There are heroes of spiritual life who, when confronted with what they have long desired, turn away and keep on pursuing the goal. Buddha renounced wife, child, father, wealth, and kingdom. Renunciation is an essential trait of the successful spiritual quest. "Whosoever he be of you that forsaketh not all that he hath, he cannot be my disciple," said Jesus (Luke 14:33). And: "Whosoever shall seek to save his life shall lose it; and whosoever shall lose his life shall preserve it" (Luke 17:33).

And others fell on the good soil and it produced good fruit: it bore sixty per measure and a hundred and twenty per measure. As the saying goes, the proof of the pudding is in the eating, and as my dear friend, the healer Ben Bibb, frequently said: "You can't argue with results." As the renowned Dr. Bronner said on his product labels: "Judge only by the amazing results."

The proof that the soil was good consisted of only one thing: the seeds produced good fruit. For lifetimes people bang away at religious dicta and get absolutely nowhere, yet they remain loyal. Today huge numbers of people follow worthless gurus and practice yoga that either does nothing significant or even harms them mentally and physically, yet they remain almost hysterically loyal. They refuse to look at the results, or lack thereof. Of course, starting out with plenty of negative conditioning–usually from religion–they are disposed to lay the blame on themselves.

Stripping away the nonsense, the principle is plain: good soil produces good fruit, both physically and metaphysically. We should never forget this simple criterion.

Yes, sometimes the results depend on the individual, so Jesus says that the amount of good fruit may vary from person to person. *But when there is good soil they all bear good fruit, and that is what matters.* Spiritual life is not a competition. Someone may have striven for lifetimes and so in this life produces a spiritual bumper crop relatively quickly, whereas another may just be beginning and will produce much less. But this has nothing to do with superior or inferior–only how long they have been working at inner cultivation.

The important thing is to note that Jesus never said that some seed bore no fruit because it was bad or unworthy. There is no place here for laying blame on the yogi. For we are all inherently divine, and in the right soil only divinity will manifest.

Divinity is within us, we only need to provide the right environment for it to come forth.

GUARDING THE FLAME

Jesus said, I have cast fire upon the world, and see, I am guarding it until it blazes. (10)

Fire

In the East fire is not regarded as a mere source of heat, but of transformation. It is further believed that fire's natural or proper abode is in the higher regions, and that it has the power to transfer material substances into those regions by reducing them to their subtle components. This concept is the basis of the Vedic fire sacrifices and is found in other religions where candles and lamps are offered before sacred depictions and in places of worship. A great number of Vedic hymns are addressed to Agni (fire) as the mouth of divinity, the gateway to supernal existence.

Tapasya

It is no surprise then that the ancient yogis spoke of spiritual practice as tapasya–the generation of heat (tapa). Especially through meditation we enkindle the fire of divine consciousness. The Shvetashvatara Upanishad speaks of it in this way: "As the form of fire when latent in its source is not seen and yet its seed is not destroyed, but may be seized again and again in its source by means of the drill [a pointed stick whirled to produce fire for the Vedic sacrifices], so it is in both cases. The Self has to be seized in the body.... By practicing the friction of meditation one may see the hidden God, as it were" (Svetasvatara Upanishad 1:13). "Practicing the friction of meditation, one should apply himself to the best of his strength" (Dhyanabindu Upanishad 22-23). "The accomplished adept completely burns up and reduces to ashes his ignorance of the atman" (Kaivalya Upanishad 11).

Meditation is thus the fire which transfers our consciousness unto the heights.

The mission of Jesus

In the context of what we have just been considering, we can see that Jesus did not come to teach a dogmatic philosophy or reveal himself as a new god to be worshipped. Rather he came to establish a way, a means, to realize God. He was a yogi come to teach yoga to questing souls. He was truly "guarding it until it blazes," though in time much of the fire was lost. Yet it still shines in the world.

Guarding our own fire

We must enkindle and then guard our own fire until it blazes forth in divine illumination. Like Jesus we must say: "My Father worketh hitherto, and I work" (John 5:17). And like Saint Paul: "We are labourers together with God" (I Corinthians 3:9).

For "The path of the just is as the shining light, that shineth more and more unto the perfect day" (Proverbs 4:18).

WHAT WILL YOU DO?

Jesus said, This heaven will pass away, and the one above it
will pass away. The dead are not alive, and the living will not
die. In the days when you consumed what is dead, you made it
what is alive. When you come to dwell in the light, what will
you do? On the day when you were one you became two. But
when you become two, what will you do? (11)

This is one of many saying of Jesus recorded in the Gospel of Thomas
which is completely inexplicable without some knowledge of Indian
philosophy (Sanatana Dharma). To me it is another demonstration of
the fact that if anyone wishes to follow Jesus they must follow him to
India for complete understanding. As a Saint Thomas Christian priest
from India once remarked to me: "To understand the teachings of Jesus
you have to know the scriptures of India."

This heaven will pass away, and the one above it will pass away. Creation takes place in cycles–projection and withdrawal–in fact, there is
no such thing as creation, but rather there is manifestation. In Sanskrit
the word for the withdrawal of the worlds is *pralaya*, which means
dissolution. The three lower worlds (lokas) or spheres are known as
Bhur, Bhuvah, and Swah. Bhu Loka is the material level of existence,

whereas Bhuvah and Swah are the two lower astral worlds, "heaven" and "the one above" that.

Jesus wants us to realize that not only is the earth temporary, so also is heaven. Neither heaven nor earth are our true home, so we must look beyond them. One Pentecost I was visiting the Coptic monastery outside Frankfort, Germany. The Abbot, Father Matthew, explained to the people that they were mistaken if they planned to go to heaven forever. "God has something much better than that," he told them. "He intends for us to enter into the great Light of God–into himself." That is why Jesus in his life as David sang: "When I awake, I am still with thee" (Psalms 139:18). And: "I will behold thy face in righteousness: I shall be satisfied, when I awake, with thy likeness" (Psalms 17:15). We must identify with our eternal nature.

The dead are not alive, and the living will not die. Jesus brings to his hearers the immortal teaching of the Bhagavad Gita: "Truly there never was a time when I was not, nor you, nor these lords of men–nor in the future will there be a time when we shall cease to be. It is known that the unreal never comes to be, and the real never ceases to be. The certainty of both of these principles is seen by those who see the truth. Know indeed that That by which all this universe is pervaded is indestructible. There is no one whatsoever capable of the destruction of the Eternal. These bodies inhabited by the eternal, indestructible, immeasurable, embodied Self are said to come to an end." (Bhagavad Gita 2:12, 16-18). Forgetting our true Selves whose very nature is Life, we identify with the material body and material conditions. We avidly run after them. Practically speaking, we pursue death and deny life, seeking to vivify the dead and kill the living: our own Self. In time, though, our true Self breaks through and posits the question the angel asked the mourners at the tomb of Jesus: "Why seek ye the living among the dead?" (Luke 24:5). Yes; why, indeed?

In the days when you consumed what is dead, you made it what is alive. We must come to realize that we are life itself, as is God, that the dead only "live" through contact with us. We are the only source of life in our private sphere of evolution. Yet we idolize that which has no value or meaning except in its relation to us. Our involvement with it is the only life it has, yet we exalt it above us and even claim to be dominated by it. In time we come to think that if it is eliminated from our life we will die, either physically or metaphysically. We are thus truly negative: black is white and white is black; empty is full and full is empty; something is nothing and nothing is something; the dead is alive and the live is dead.

The dilemma is colossal. How can we ever break out of it? Actually it is easy because we are Life itself. All we need do is turn to our own Self. That is why Buddha said: "Turn around, and behold! the Other Shore." Getting into our mess is much harder than getting out. This is an unaccepted truth, but it is no less the truth. It is material life that is hard, because it is an attempt to accomplish the impossible, to make the dead alive. Spiritual life is comparatively easy because it is a matter of "is"–of eternal reality.

Our eternal status must be pursued, must be driven home in our consciousness. So Jesus puts forth two crucial questions.

When you come to dwell in the light, what will you do? When our consciousness once more comes to dwell in the light of spirit, both finite and Infinite, what will we do? Nothing. As Buddha said: "Birth is exhausted [that is, the karma that produces birth is dissolved, has ceased to exist], the holy life has been lived out, what can be done is done, of this there is no more beyond." Perfection having been reentered, nothing remains to be done or not done.

On the day when you were one you became two. But when you become two, what will you do? There was a time when we were in the state of unity, but then we entered into duality. When that occurred, what, then, could we do? Again: nothing. For we had made ourselves helpless through immersion in unreality.

There is, however, a single thing needed: Awakening. But we do not "do" awakening, for being awake is a state. So we need only stop sleeping and lo! we will find ourselves awake in Reality. Therefore Saint Paul wrote: "Awake, thou that sleepest, and arise from the dead, and Christ shall give thee light" (Ephesians 5:14).

WHO SHALL LEAD?

The disciples said to Jesus, We know that you will depart from us. Who is to be our leader? Jesus said to them, Wherever you are, you are to go to James the righteous, for whose sake heaven and earth came into being. (12)

Somehow this section was missing from the text of the translation I used in commenting, so it was missing from the first printing. Fortunately someone wrote asking about James the Just (in this translation called "the Righteous"). As a result I spent a good deal of time looking into the various historical accounts still used today in the Christian East regarding the three apostles named James: James the Great, James the Brother of the Lord and James the Just. What I found was much confusion. What was found in the life of one disciple was often found in that of another—or even of all three. Untangling this confusion is impossible, so I will not even attempt to say which James is being referred to here.

What is significant is Jesus' advice to seek guidance from one of the Jameses and not Saint Peter whom the West calls "Prince of the Apostles" and claim was the head of the apostolic Church. It also reveals that no one can determine much of the character of Christianity in its primal days.

For this reason I go to *The Aquarian Gospel of Jesus the Christ* by Levi Dowling and the writings of Paramhansa Yogananda, especially *The Second Coming of Christ*, to find out what Jesus really did and taught.

Certainly in the Aquarian Gospel we find that Peter, James and John (the two sons of Zebedee, called "the Sons of Thunder" by Jesus) had a definite spiritual primacy in the sight of Jesus. On the night of his arrest, Jesus took Peter, James and John apart and spoke to them of many divine mysteries, saying at one point: "You, my three, who constitute the inner circle of the Church of Christ, will show to men the attributes of all the Gods. And Peter shall make known the Power of God; and James shall show the Thought of God; and John shall demonstrate the Love of God" (164:42-44).

THE UNSPEAKABLE

"I know the departed beings and the living, and those who are yet to be, but none whatsoever knows me" (Bhagavad Gita 7:26). So said Krishna on the battlefield. Then later:

> Jesus said to his disciples, Compare me to someone and tell me whom I am like.
>
> Simon Peter said to him, 'You are like a righteous angel.'
>
> Matthew said to him, 'You are like a wise philosopher.'
>
> Thomas said to him, 'Master, my mouth is wholly incapable of saying whom you are like.'
>
> Jesus said, 'I am not your master. Because you have drunk, you have become intoxicated from the bubbling spring which I have measured out.'
>
> And he took him and withdrew and told him three things. When Thomas returned to his companions, they asked him, 'What did Jesus say to you?'
>
> Thomas said to them, 'If I tell you one of the things which he told me, you will pick up stones and throw them at me; a fire will come out of the stones and burn you up.' (13)

Levels of consciousness, levels of understanding

It is sometimes said in the East that there are as many worlds as there are human beings–that we each see the world according to the level of our consciousness, which is greatly–usually totally–subjective. I saw this early on in my life. I knew people who lived and breathed the supernatural. They did not believe in spiritual realities, they knew them. (As Jung once told an interviewer: "I do not *believe* there is a God, I *know* there is a God.") Yet right next door to them lived people who had not a hint of anything beyond the "normal" mundane life. It is a matter of record that some people can enter a haunted place and instantly be aware of its character, whereas others can even live there and experience nothing unusual.

Perception is a matter of evolution, and so is understanding. In the Bhagavad Gita and the Gospels there are expositions of how people perceive things according to their capacity for insight. The same is true in this incident from the Gospel of Thomas. Peter, being emotional and sentimental, thinks Jesus is a holy angel. Matthew, more intellectual, sees him as a worthy philosopher. But Thomas, having a mystical outlook derived from experience, knows that he cannot intellectually express the nature of Jesus. In Eastern Christianity they adamantly say that God cannot be seen–and that you will know it when you see him! What they mean is that God cannot be encompassed by the finite mind of the individual, yet Divinity can be perceived to some degree. No one standing on the shore can see the ocean in the sense of seeing the whole thing. We can only see a tiny bit of the ocean. So we both do and do not see it, like the person who, dazzled by the sun, says: "I can't see anything." But of course he sees the bright sunlight.

This is why they also say in the East: "He who knows tells it not; he who tells knows it not."

No longer "master"

In response to Thomas's words, Jesus tells him that he is no longer his master, for Thomas has drunk of the same font from which he drew his wisdom. Even though contemporary Christianity insists on us being servants of Jesus, grovelling before him as not just our master but our God, Jesus said to his original disciples: "I call you not servants; for the servant knoweth not what his lord doeth: but I have called you friends; for all things that I have heard of my Father I have made known unto you" (John 15:15). Now they, too, were knowers (gnostics) as was Jesus. And we can be the same.

Brown translates Jesus' words as: "I am not your teacher, now that you have drunk. You have become drunken from the bubbling spring which I have measured out." This is like the eleventh Ode of Solomon which says: "Speaking waters drew near my lips, from the fountain of the Lord plenteously. And I drank and was inebriated with the living waters that do not die. And my inebriation was not one without knowledge, but I forsook vanity" (Odes of Solomon 11:6-8).

The disciples of Jesus ceased to be disciples and became his friends. It would seem that there is a great difference between being a Christian and being a friend of Christ, a true disciple. Rather than wailing over the wicked world and warning everyone to "flee from the wrath to come," Jesus' friends rejoice in the life they have found. And share it.

Just a few hours before beginning to write this article, I read some of the reminiscences of Sri Ma Sarada Devi by Ashutosh Mitra, a disciple of Sri Ma and brother of Sri Ramakrishna's disciple Swami Trigunatitananda who lived many years in San Francisco. He told of how he met a young doctor who was addicted to alcohol and drugs because of the great sorrows of his life. When the doctor told Ashutosh of his sufferings, Ashutosh assured him that he (Ashutosh) knew the way to great happiness and the end of all grief. After some time he took the doctor to meet the Holy Mother Sarada Devi, who gave him, too, the secret of a blessed life. He no longer needed faith; she had shown him the living way, the real way of Christ—and of Buddha and Krishna, as well.

The wisdom of "unknowing"

Because Thomas knew that Reality is beyond limited human speech, Jesus could teach him the real Gospel–the Good News. This is one of the contradictions with which human existence abounds. Those who know they cannot know are then enabled to know.

Whether Jesus only spoke three actual words, or whether he spoke three sentences or even three discourses, we cannot know, for *logos* means all three of those things. But whichever it may have been, they were mighty in their effect. For when the others asked what he had been taught, Thomas assured them that they would stone him for blasphemy if he told them even one part. Or rather, they would try to stone him but would themselves be destroyed for their rashness. For Truth destroys untruth–sometimes even on the material level, just as Uzzah was killed when he touched the Ark of the Covenant, being virtually electrocuted by the tremendous power that pulsed through it (II Samuel 6:3-7), which is why it could only be carried by means of poles put through the metal rings on its sides.

Spiritual realities are not always reassuring or even safe to the ignorant. And there Saint Thomas leaves the whole matter.

WHEN VIRTUE IS VICE

Jesus said to them, If you fast, you will give rise to sin for yourselves; and if you pray, you will be condemned; and if you give alms, you will do harm to your spirits. (14)

There is a Zen story of a man who gave an answer to a roshi's question, and was told he had answered correctly. The next day the roshi asked the same question and the man gave the same answer. The roshi said his answer was wrong. When the man protested that the day before his answer was said to be correct, the roshi replied that the day before it had been right, but today it was wrong. The idea was that as we move forward in consciousness, Yes can become No, No can become Yes, and both can become Neither.

In the Father's "house" are many "mansions" (John 14:2). In the field of relative existence, there are many strata, many realities. As a consequence, what is wise in one stratum can be folly in another. This is expressed in this verse of the Gospel of Thomas. Obviously, fasting, prayer, and almsgiving are viable forms of self-purification. But Jesus is leading the disciples to a higher realm, a higher understanding, in which those things are no longer relevant.

Fasting

Fasting is purely physical. Being in a material body, we are deeply influenced by its conditions and changes. The mind and body are so interwoven they are often indistinguishable. Therefore our eating patterns affect us greatly. Fasting is recommended as a means of lessening our body identity. This is certainly beneficial. But once a person develops skill in yoga, his center of awareness is shifted into higher mental levels, and a physical practice no longer has the efficacy it once had. In time it becomes irrelevant. A point is reached in which fasting is as silly as having a horse pull an automobile rather than turning on the engine. Therefore to continue fasting as a spiritual discipline is to act incongruously with our present status and can, through habit, cause us to revert to our former status in which fasting was relevant. So what was once an aid can become a detriment.

Prayer

It is the same with prayer. It presupposes the absurdity that we need to inform God of our inner thoughts, feelings, and needs–that otherwise he will either not know of them or will not care about them. Furthermore, prayer assumes a dependency on another and denies our own innate power as spiritual beings. Jesus frequently told people that it was their faith, their conviction, that healed them (Matthew 9:22, 15:28; Mark 5:34, 10:52; Luke 7:50, 8:48, 17:19, 18:42). Yet, we steadfastly refuse to believe this fundamental truth: "According to your faith be it unto you" (Matthew 9:29).

In Greek, the language of the Four Gospels and parts of the Gospel of Thomas, two words are used which in English are translated "prayer." One is *deesis*, which means asking for something. This is what Jesus condemns in this instance. The second word is *prosevke*, which means "to draw near." This is a completely different matter, as it is a spiritual movement toward infinity. Even verbal formulas can effect this drawing near to higher consciousness. This form of prayer is not being censured by Jesus.

The much worse aspect of prayer (deesis) is its presupposition that we are separate from God. So when we pray we affirm this illusion and strengthen ourselves in it. The Chandogya Upanishad tells us: "Where one sees nothing else, hears nothing else, understands nothing else, that is the infinite. But where one sees something else, hears something else, understands something else, that is the small [the finite]. Verily, the infinite is the same as the immortal, the finite is the same as the mortal" (Chandogya Upanishad 24:1). To affirm a non-existent separation from God is to doom ourselves to mortality, to death-in-life.

Almsgiving

The situation is very much the same with almsgiving, if we see those we give assistance to as separate from ourselves. When we help others we are really helping ourselves, for in God we are at one with all that lives. Not only that, those with opened spiritual eyes see that whatever they do to others they do to God, the Indweller of Hearts (Matthew 25:40; Bhagavad Gita 10:20; 15:15, 17; 18:61). Through others we either give or take from God. This is an awesome truth. If God is the object of our almsgiving, then it is an act of supreme virtue that leads to the Supreme.

What to do?

Should we then immediately stop these three observances? Not necessarily. What is needed is for us to diligently apply ourselves to meditation and rectitude of life so we can ascend to that level of evolution in which the words of Jesus apply to us just as they did to the apostles.

Father in Heaven;
Father on Earth

Jesus said, When you see one who was not born of woman, prostrate yourselves on your faces and worship him. That one is your father. (15)

Everyone who has read the Gospels is very familiar with the injunction: "Call no man your father upon the earth: for one is your Father, which is in heaven" (Matthew 23:9). I grew up with this verse being used as a stone to throw at Catholics for calling a priest "Father" while the stone-throwers proceeded to write in their biological father's name on all kinds of forms and applications. Bigotry is its own justification.

However that might be, when we turn to the East and even the yoga world this mandate goes out the window in a welter of adulation and titles. One time at a spiritual conference in Northern India I heard a shameless and (literally) criminal guru even more shamelessly being introduced with a string of inflated titles that went on for a long time before his name was even reached. A friend of mine came across several lines of adulatory appellations in reference to a contemporary super-guru who claimed to be the only legitimate guru presently on the earth. "Why don't they just call him 'God'?" he demanded in disgust. "It would be easier to spell and shorter to say!" Of course a lot of "avatars" are presently racing around India and the world. What to do about it? Nothing. Let them and their followers have their fun. And let us consider what real masters have taught–such as this verse from the Gospel of Thomas.

Since only God is our Father (and Mother), only God, or someone who is totally one with God and knows that God is his Self, can be called (or considered) Father in the spiritual sense. Jesus obviously has no problem with calling God Father, but this verse is obviously referring to human beings, or at least those in human form.

He is quite simple in his exposition. "One who was not born of woman" is Father. "Woman" has two levels of meaning in this: 1) humanity and 2) the cosmos–relativity itself. So a "Father" can have no identity with either limited humanity or the human body. That is, he knows himself as neither the body nor even human. Further, he does not in any way consider himself to be an entity separate from God, however exalted that status might be. He sees and knows only the Absolute. Even his individual Self he knows only in its eternal relation to God. Creation (Prakriti) has ceased to exist for him and only the consciousness of Spirit (Purusha) prevails. Nothing about him has been born from anything but the Infinite.

When we do meet such a one, they are worthy of reverence and even worship to some extent. (It should be pointed out here that such a Father may be in female form.)

The big question is Who? Who is such a divinized being? Naturally everyone is going to insist their guru or other kind of religious potentate is such a one, and there is no reasoning with them. I could give my list, but what value is that? The problem lies in the subjectivity that has to come into such opinions.

The best thing is not to care, but to keep on making sure we ourselves become such a one in the future.

DIVINE DISCORD

Jesus said, Men think, perhaps, that it is peace which I have come to cast upon the world. They do not know that it is dissension which I have come to cast upon the earth: fire, sword, and war. For there will be five in a house: three will be against two, and two against three, the father against the son, and the son against the father. And they will stand solitary. (16)

Men think, perhaps, that it is peace which I have come to cast upon the world. Yogananda remarked that human beings are skillful in their ignorance–especially in maintaining and justifying it. In religion this is supremely true. As I have pointed out elsewhere, the motto of all religions based on an avatar or prophet seems to be: "Ignore the message and adore the messenger." One of the most amazing examples of this is the way Buddhists manage to ignore the fact that Buddha said his dharma would have vanished from the earth within five centuries after him. Another is the Prince of Peace slogan that we hear every Christmas, even though Jesus himself said: "I am come to send fire on the earth; and what will I, if it be already kindled? Suppose ye that I am come to give peace on earth? I tell you, Nay; but rather division: for from henceforth there shall be five in one house divided, three against two, and two against three. The father shall be divided against the son, and the son against the father; the mother against the daughter, and the daughter against the mother; the mother in law against her daughter in law, and the daughter in law against her mother in law" (Luke 12:49-53).

And what about these predictions he made regarding his disciples? "Then shall they deliver you up to be afflicted, and shall kill you: and ye shall be hated of all nations for my name's sake" (Matthew 24:9). "Blessed are ye, when men shall hate you, and when they shall separate you from their company, and shall reproach you, and cast out your name as evil, for the Son of man's sake" (Luke 6:22). "The time cometh, that whosoever killeth you will think that he doeth God service" (John 16:2). If this is "God's peace plan," what is his war plan?

They do not know that it is dissension which I have come to cast upon the earth: fire, sword, and war. Jesus, who said: "the words that I speak unto you, are spirit" (John 6:63), meant fire, sword, and war in a purely symbolic sense–as spiritual symbols. Fire is tapasya (don't forget, Jesus had spent most of his life in India). Sword is the will directed to vanquish inner negativity and ignorance. War is the great conflict, the fight unto death with ignorance and bondage, the transmutation of mortality into immortality. The "judgement" presented in the book of Revelation is a purely internal phenomenon that takes place when the process of spiritual alchemy becomes dominant and enters the final stages. It is awesome– and awful–and requires intense will-power to maintain. It is riding the tiger: fall off and you get eaten. This is why there is no place in authentic spiritual life for sentimentality masquerading as devotion and weakness masquerading as gentleness and humility. Jesus said it quite plainly: "The kingdom of heaven suffereth violence, and the violent take it by force" (Matthew 11:12). That is why the Gita is spoken on a battlefield. And also why the largest amounts of saints in any religion have arisen in imperialist and militarily-oriented cultures. Having imbibed the strength, courage, and determination of those cultures, they transmuted them into spiritual powers within themselves and thus won the inner kingdom.

For there will be five in a house: three will be against two, and two against three, the father against the son, and the son against the father. Jesus also said: "A man's foes shall be they of his own household" (Matthew 10:36). Painful as this is on both sides, it is not at all uncommon that those closest to us will oppose our spiritual life. Yet we must persevere. In time there may be reconciliation and even appreciation. (In some cases the opponents become convinced of the value of spiritual life and take it up themselves.) Often it is society that is the opponent, and things can get extremely petty and extremely vicious. Courage is needed. This is even more true when the conflicts are internal, when we are at war with ourselves.

One of the most spiritually gifted persons I have known was also extremely caught up in pure idiocy. It was really grievous to see this great soul bound to such meaningless values. Destruction seemed so inevitable, and yet she would have been a saint in this life if she had only shaken them loose. Through the years I have seen so many evolved and worthy people cursed with spiritual schizophrenia. Those that were in conflict at least had some hope, but most were going right along with their inner enemies, harming themselves with each day of neglect. The enemy outside can always be resisted, but what of the enemy within?

There is a hint here of the subtle anatomy of the human being. We are composed of five concentric sheaths or bodies (koshas): the anna-maya (physical), pranamaya (life-force), manomaya (mind), jnanamaya (intellect), and anandamaya (bliss) bodies respectively. The three lower–annamaya, pranamaya and manomaya bodies are called "the earth" and the two above–jnanamaya and anandamaya–are "heaven." In an evolved person there is a necessary antagonism between the three and the two–just as Jesus says. This conflict arises only when a goodly level of inner growth has occurred. Simply stated, the three lower bodies are the realm of material consciousness and the two upper bodies deal with higher feelings and perceptions, especially intelligence and will power. Whereas the three lower bodies have no spiritual aspects, the upper two can be either merely human or a mixture of humanity and spirituality. These two become dominantly spiritual when the requisite level of evolution is attained. Then spiritual life becomes much easier and success becomes inevitable through perseverance.

When this yogic knowledge is possessed by the seeker, spiritual life becomes an altogether different matter than before. The torment, frustration, and confusion that can overwhelm the struggling seeker who is unaware of the real facts of spiritual life is absolutely terrible. I speak from personal experience and observation of others. For years I lived in a low-level hell of doubt and fear in the midst of exuberant happy-time Fundamentalism. I seemed to have a spiritual life, and even had what seemed to be spiritual experience. But like the young man in the Gospel I cried out: "What lack I yet?" (Matthew 19:20). All around me I saw people who had the same dilemma, but they all gave up in one form or another. Most suppressed their inner voice, drowning it out with loud professions of faith and trust, and in time their heart's monitor was silenced. Others dropped out totally and became enmeshed in the crassest and most tedious aspects of material life. A few desolate souls kept on trying, consulting every new minister, hitting the "mourner's bench" at every revival, consulting in desperation any person or book they thought might help. They fasted, prayed, and even travelled to other places seeking help. They cried out for peace, but there was no peace. I have known some who believed they had committed "the sin against the Holy Spirit" and were irrevocably damned. I am sorry to say that I do not know of a single one who eventually managed.

Well, I know of one: myself. Walking by a drugstore one day I saw a brightly-colored cover on one of the book racks. Afraid of being late for school, I went on, but that afternoon on the way home I went in and looked at it. In my dimness I did not realize what it was, even though I had hoped it would be a book on spiritual matters—a hope that must have really been an intuition. Because of the blurb on the back and the format of much of the text, I thought it was only an ancient poem.

My disappointment was really sharp, and every day when I passed by I would look in and see the book and wish it had been what I had hoped. Nearly seven years later I bought the book at a college book store, read it, and experienced a life-change I would not have believed possible. That little book was *Bhagavad Gita: The Song of God* translated by Swami Prabhavananda. Next I read *Autobiography of a Yogi,* which gave coherency and direction to my new life. I cannot say the rest is history because it is still going on.

The immense relief I experienced when through those two books I understood what had been happening to me cannot be expressed. The inner enemies were identified and their nature revealed along with the knowledge of how to vanquish them. It would take a lot of work, *but at last I knew what I was doing.* Confusion, fear, and doubt were over. I had become a yogi. And I knew what Jesus meant when he told his disciples: "Peace I leave with you, my peace I give unto you: not as the world giveth, give I unto you. Let not your heart be troubled, neither let it be afraid" (John 14:27). Here is how I wrote about it some years back:

"In the late afternoon a day or so after finishing *Autobiography of a Yogi,* just as dusk was coming on I was pondering the revelations I had received from my reading while at the same time getting ready to go out with my parents and some of their friends. Suddenly I felt a great peace descend upon–and within–me. It was the 'good and perfect gift from above, coming down from the Father of Lights,' of that I had no doubt. I realized that for the first time in this life I was finding out what it was to be truly blessed. Although I was absorbed in my extraordinary experience, I was able to behave as usual.

"A couple of hours later as I sat in a restaurant savoring my inner banquet, the words came into my mind: 'You do not hurt inside any more,' referring to the internal pain that had been with me without interruption since my mother's death. My grief had not only been inexpressible, it had proven ineradicable. I never got over my mother's death, but continued to mourn through the years. Naturally, in order to function with a semblance of normality I had to submerge my interior suffering beneath my ordinary consciousness. I learned to genuinely laugh and enjoy things, but if I became very still and turned my awareness inside I would find a continuous sorrow flowing within me. Inwardly I shed perpetual tears of desolation.

"As I say, I had adjusted to this through the years, so to be told by some mysterious intuition that I no longer had any inner anguish was the most incredible idea that could have occurred to me. Yet it was true. I turned my attention within and probed around. Profound peace alone was to be encountered. I was healed. It was as simple as that. Equally simple was my conviction that this healing had come from Yogananda himself. My gratitude and amazement were equally without limit."

And they will stand solitary. Some translations have: "And they will stand alone." Both the spiritual aspirants and their opponents will "stand solitary." The aspirants will find that except for God they can rely on no one but themselves, that if help does not come from within there will be no help at all. Even the wisdom of great masters means nothing it we do not apply it diligently. This is why we can apply to spiritual life the popular saying about the Westward expansion in America: "The cowards never started; the weak died along the way." The opponents will "stand alone" in that they will be totally and solely responsible for trying to destroy the spiritual life of another. And in time they will be the opposed themselves, for what they sow they reap.

False teachers promise effortless attainment, the most shameless of them even claiming: "I have done it for you already," and insisting that their dupes need only "surrender" to them. Rare are the honest teachers like Jesus who will spell out what the seeker can expect. Only the true teachers believe in the seekers' capacity to succeed by their own divine nature and power. A sensible gardener knows that however much the soil is prepared and watered, the seeds grow only from within, actualizing their inherent nature. It is the same with human beings.

THE DIVINE GIFT

Jesus said, I shall give you what no eye has seen and what no ear has heard and what no hand has touched and what has never occurred to the human mind. (17)

We are familiar with this idea from Saint Paul's saying: "It is written, Eye hath not seen, nor ear heard, neither have entered into the heart of man, the things which God hath prepared for them that love him" (I Corinthians 2:9). He was quoting Isaiah 64:4: "For since the beginning of the world men have not heard, nor perceived by the ear, neither hath the eye seen, O God, beside thee, what he hath prepared for him that waiteth for him."

The King James translation misses the idea a bit. The original Greek actually says: "What eye has not seen and ear has not heard, *and to which the heart of man has not aspired,* that has God prepared for those that love Him." Naturally the heart of "man" has not aspired to the divine gift, because it is far beyond the grasp of the earthbound mind and heart of those entrenched in the human condition, having forgotten that they are gods and not men. ("I have said, Ye are gods; and all of you are children of the most High" Psalms 82:6.)

It takes a moderate degree of evolution to realize that there is a realm that is invisible to the eye, unheard by the ear, untouchable to the hand and beyond the imagining of the human mind. But it takes a great degree of evolution to understand that that realm is the real world, and that we are living in a mirage, a dream—which has meaning, but is nonetheless a dream. To aspire to enter that true world and leave this world of mere appearance is a mark of nearness to the status of "the sons of God." And that is the gift Jesus offers to His disciples, the real Christmas gift that comes to us when we are born into the real world of God.

THE ORIGIN IS THE END

> The disciples said to Jesus, Tell us how our end will be. Jesus said, Have you discovered, then, the beginning, that you look for the end? For where the beginning is, there will the end be. Blessed is he who will take his place in the beginning; he will know the end and will not experience death. (18)

Tell us how our end will be. Those who believe firmly in their mortality are obsessed by two things: 1) When will they die? and 2) When will the world end? This reveals that however metaphysically some of them may talk, they know only this world as reality and the animation of a body as life. Material consciousness prevails in most religion—it is difficult indeed to find those who "walk in the spirit" (Galatians 5:16, 25). Considering that at the very moment of Jesus' departure from them the Apostles still had no understanding of the nature of the Kingdom (Acts 1:6), it is small wonder that earlier they asked about their "end." This is why on the eve of his passion, Jesus said: "Have I been so long time with you, and yet hast thou not known me?" (John 14:9).

Have you discovered, then, the beginning, that you look for the end? The word in the Greek text is "origin" not "beginning." This is a significant distinction, for the origin of all is God himself. We must transcend time and enter into the eternal. Unless we do that, we can know nothing about anything.

Where the beginning is, there will the end be. Time and space are fundamental illusions, therefore the origin, the beginning and the end are simultaneous–but only in God. Outside God we will see it very differently–and wrongly. So to know the truth of these matters we must become totally identified with reality, united to God in the permanent consciousness of unity.

Blessed is he who will take his place in the beginning; he will know the end and will not experience death. Those who return to the Origin and become established in that Consciousness will know the end, because the return is itself the end. Such a one shall never undergo death. As Emily Bronte wrote:

No coward soul is mine,
No trembler in the world's storm-troubled sphere:
I see Heaven's glories shine,
And Faith shines equal, arming me from Fear.

O God within my breast,
Almighty, ever-present Deity!
Life, that in me has rest,
As I, undying Life, have power in Thee!

Vain are the thousand creeds
That move men's hearts: unutterably vain;
Worthless as withered weeds,
Or idlest froth amid the boundless main,

To waken doubt in one
Holding so fast by Thy infinity,
So surely anchored on
The steadfast rock of Immortality.

With wide-embracing love
Thy Spirit animates eternal years,
Pervades and broods above,
Changes, sustains, dissolves, creates, and rears.

Though earth and moon were gone,
And suns and universes ceased to be,
And Thou wert left alone,
Every existence would exist in Thee.

There is not room for Death,
Nor atom that his might could render void:
Thou—thou art Being and Breath,
And what thou art may never be destroyed.

Original Being

Jesus said, 'Blessed is he who came into being before he came into being. If you become my disciples and listen to my words, these stones will minister to you. For there are five trees for you in Paradise which remain undisturbed summer and winter and whose leaves do not fall. Whoever becomes acquainted with them will not experience death.' (19)

Blessed is he who came into being before he came into being. This can also be translated: "Blessed is he who was before he came into being." In the Gospel of Saint John Jesus prays: "O Father, glorify thou me with thine own self with the glory which I had with thee before the world was" (John 17:5). Jesus is saying that those who remember that glory and are again established in it are blessed for they are living in the vision and being of God. And like him they can say: "I and my Father are one" (John 10:30). Once a contemporary mystic was asked how to meditate. He replied: "Go back to before the world existed." If we do that we will know God and our own Self.

If you become my disciples and listen to my words, these stones will minister to you. All creation will assist us in our search for divine perfection. It is not the material world that is our enemy, but the false intellectual and spiritual world of human ignorance. When we realize that God is manifesting as all the creation, how could we think otherwise? Since the material world is in harmony with God and man, Jesus said: "God is able of these stones to raise up children unto Abraham" (Matthew 3:9). "And he answered and said unto them, I tell you that, if these should hold their peace, the stones would immediately cry out" (Luke 19:40). Consciousness is inherent in all material things. The world will not hold us back, but "man" certainly will.

For there are five trees for you in Paradise which remain undisturbed summer and winter and whose leaves do not fall. Whoever becomes acquainted with them will not experience death. I have always admired people who knew their limitations and acknowledged them. So I must follow my own ideals by admitting that I cannot say what this means. Some translators speculate that Jesus is speaking of the five senses, but their acquaintance hardly bestows immortality.

A Mustard Seed

The disciples said to Jesus, Tell us what the kingdom of
heaven is like. He said to them, It is like a mustard seed. It
is the smallest of all seeds. But when it falls on tilled soil, it
produces a great plant and becomes a shelter for birds of the
sky. (20)

The word translated "heaven" is *ouranos*, the sky, which represents the
boundless Consciousness that is God. In Sanskrit texts it is known
as the Chidakasha, the Conscious Ether which pervades all things and
is the support of their existence because they are all formed of it. So
the kingdom of heaven is the kingdom of infinite being which is also
infinite consciousness. It is this level of existence that we must enter
into, leaving all other levels behind. That is, we must rise from relative
consciousness into the divine consciousness that is our true essential
being. That is why we pray:

Lead me from the unreal to the Real;
Lead me from darkness to the Light;
Lead me from death to Immortality.

In American slang we sometimes say to someone: "Get real!" and that is what Jesus is saying to us.

Jesus is indicating that since all things are formed of consciousness (chinmaya), infinity is inherent in the finite, that from finite consciousness comes infinite consciousness just as from infinite consciousness has arisen the finite consciousness. Since that is the origin of the finite, infinite consciousness is inherent in the finite consciousness. We need only cultivate the seed of our own consciousness to attain infinity. Though small in its scope, the individual spirit-consciousness can become limitless, embracing all forms of existence.

But it will do so only "when it falls on tilled soil." The various bodies of the yogi are like the soil; they must be cultivated assiduously and-hanged in their character, otherwise the seed of consciousness will not sprout and grow. It will remain as limited and confined as always. It does not matter how religious we are, how much good deeds we perform, or even how much spiritual study we engage in.

Our bodies are formed of the vibrating energy known as prakriti. In the Bhagavad Gita we are told: "One acts according to one's own prakriti–even the wise man does so. Beings follow their own prakriti; what will restraint accomplish?" (Bhagavad Gita 3:33). Therefore external behavior accomplishes very little. Even moral principles only remove or prevent obstacles to higher consciousness; refinement and evolution of our prakriti is the necessary element, without which nothing real and lasting will occur.

Since "the kingdom of God is within you" (Luke 17:21), it is a matter of internal development and opening.

DISCIPLES OF JESUS

Mary said to Jesus, Whom are your disciples like? He said,
They are like children who have settled in a field which is not
theirs. When the owners of the field come, they will say, Let
us have back our field. They (will) undress in their presence in
order to let them have back their field and to give it back to
them. Therefore I say, if the owner of a house knows that the
thief is coming, he will begin his vigil before he comes and will
not let him dig through into his house of his domain to carry
away his goods. You, then, be on your guard against the world.
Arm yourselves with great strength lest the robbers find a way
to come to you, for the difficulty which you expect will (surely)
materialize. Let there be among you a man of understanding.
When the grain ripened, he came quickly with his sickle in his
hand and reaped it. Whoever has ears to hear, let him hear. (21)

*Mary said to Jesus, Whom are your disciples like? He said, They are like
children who have settled in a field which is not theirs.* Saint Peter
addressed the Christians in general, calling them "strangers and pilgrims"
(I Peter 2:11), and Saint Paul said that the holy men and women of old
"confessed that they were strangers and pilgrims on the earth" (Hebrews

11:13). They were following the words of Jesus recorded here. The true disciples of Jesus know that nothing of this earth is theirs and never will be, for they are "children of the kingdom" of God Consciousness alone (Matthew 13:38). Their home is infinity, in God. As the hymn says:

Let us sing a sweet song of the home of the soul,
     The glorious place of our rest;
It is not far away in the heavens untold,
     But deep in the Infinite breast.

When the owners of the field come, they will say, Let us have back our field. They (will) undress in their presence in order to let them have back their field and to give it back to them. In commenting on the previous verse I spoke of the world as being a field, but our bodies are also fields, as indicated in the thirteenth chapter of the Bhagavad Gita entitled "The Field and Its Knower." The first verse encapsulates what follows, saying: "This body is called the Field, and he who knows this is called the Knower of the Field–so say the knowers of these things." And he does not identify with it, knowing that he is merely a witness, an immaterial spirit-consciousness.

Who, then, owns the field? God, obviously, but the owners spoken of here are those whom God has placed in charge of the creation and its evolution. They are the Elohim, the Creator Mothers, whom the first verse of Genesis tells us created heaven and earth and later said: "Let us make man in our image, after our likeness" (Genesis 1:26). Supervising our evolution which involves a series of earthly births, when the store of karma runs out for a life they come and demand that we give the body-field back to them for recycling in the universe and in preparation for our next embodiment. So we divest ourselves of the present bodies. As the Gita says: "As a man casts off his worn-out clothes and then clothes himself in others which are new, so the embodied casts off worn-out bodies and then enters into others which are new" (Bhagavad Gita

2:22). Unfortunately some who are attached to the body or fear death resist and battle the surrender of their fields, but eventually they must relinquish the body and find that they are immortal.

Therefore I say, if the owner of a house knows that the thief is coming, he will begin his vigil before he comes and will not let him dig through into his house of his domain to carry away his goods. You, then, be on your guard against the world. Arm yourselves with great strength lest the robbers find a way to come to you, for the difficulty which you expect will (surely) materialize. These words imply that it is the world–both materiality and material experience–which deceives us into identifying with our material constitution, our field, who is the thief against whom we must guard ourselves. This can only be done by viewing the world with the correct perspective while cultivating spiritual consciousness in place of earthly consciousness.

When Jesus tells us: "Lay up for yourselves treasures in heaven" (Matthew 6:20), he is not speaking of some astral world where we can reap positive karma, but the kingdom of heaven, the limitless spirit-consciousness into which we must seek to be freed, escaping forever the bondage of birth and death in this or any other world, material, astral, or causal. In other words, we lay up the treasure of spiritual realization in the infinite Life that is God. Divinity becomes our treasure-house so in time we may enter into perfect union with it. If we accumulate earthly treasure, death will snatch it from us sooner or later and we will become impoverished, but if our treasure is in the heaven of Spirit we shall never lose it.

There are many robbers who seek to plunder our spirit and its powers, so Jesus says we must exert great strength against them. Sometimes we combat them face-to-face and hand-to-hand. Who are the robbers? Anything that dims or takes from us our spiritual consciousness and imposes material consciousness on us.

Troubles will come, but Jesus assures us: "In the world ye shall have tribulation: but be of good cheer; I have overcome the world" (John 16:33). And so shall we overcome if we heed his counsels.

Let there be among you a man of understanding. When the grain ripened, he came quickly with his sickle in his hand and reaped it. Whoever has ears to hear, let him hear. "So is the kingdom of God, as if a man should cast seed into the ground; and should sleep, and rise night and day, and the seed should spring and grow up, he knoweth not how. For the earth bringeth forth fruit of herself; first the blade, then the ear, after that the full corn in the ear. But when the fruit is brought forth, immediately he putteth in the sickle, because the harvest is come" (Mark 4:26-29).

Spiritual vigilance is being urged upon us here, as in the previous verse. Spiritual heedlessness takes many forms. There are people who actually engage in spiritual practice, but for some reason do it in a rote way without examining its effects or evincing any kind of spiritual aspiration or ambition. They are rather like a friend of mine in India who worked in a bank and every payday took her salary in cash and never counted it or even knew what the amount was supposed to be. (She did not know how many pice were in a rupee, either.)

The wise spiritual aspirant must be on the constant lookout for spiritual results and opportunities for spiritual advancement, which includes increasing his spiritual practices and disciplines. Consider how vigilant and ready a good farmer or gardener must be, for they are dealing with living things that are subject to many elements that may be detrimental or beneficial. The wise farmers and gardeners must be deeply involved in their cultivation, watching for developments and acting accordingly. Our eye must always be on the exit, ready as soon as we are able to move up to the next higher level of consciousness and evolution. Those who dawdle and dally on the way may, like Little Red Riding Hood, end up in the wolf's stomach.

"He that hath ears to hear, let him hear" (Matthew 11:15).

How to Enter the Kingdom

Jesus saw infants being suckled. He said to his disciples, These infants being suckled are like those who enter the kingdom. They said to him, Shall we then, as children, enter the kingdom? Jesus said to them, When you make the two one, and when you make the inside like the outside and the outside like the inside, and the above like the below, and when you make the male and the female one and the same, so that the male not be male nor the female female; and when you fashion eyes in the place of an eye, and a hand in place of a hand, and a foot in place of a foot, and a likeness in place of a likeness; then will you enter the kingdom. (22)

When you make the two one. There never has been any thing or any state but the One. But through that mirage-power we call Maya we are immersed in the experience of duality, and from that springs all our troubles. Only when the experience of unity is established in us will we know freedom from fear and suffering. We are seeing and living defectively, constantly agitated by subject-object duality. All the philosophy in the world cannot remove an atom of our dilemma. However, it can help us to disbelieve in the duality and learn from dual experience, like someone watching a training film or doing creative visualization. For our present state of dual consciousness is not a curse or even an obstacle. It is our mistaken reaction to it that causes the problems.

I said philosophy would not help, and it will not. We must have the means to "*make* the two one." Believing in unity and affirming it over and over gets us nowhere. We must turn our perception of two into the perception of One. Since our experience of duality is an inner condition, we must employ inner correction. Going within we must remove the cataracts of misperception and clear our spirit vision. Meditation is the sole way to accomplish this, for an interior remedy is needed for an interior malady. Once the mistaken duality has disappeared and the true One appeared, we are cured of our age-long delusion and the ignorance accruing from it.

When you make the inside like the outside and the outside like the inside, and the above like the below. Part of our present trouble is inconsistency and conflict within our own complex being. "Inside" and "outside" must also be turned into a single thing along with "above" and "below," for these distinctions are fundamentally erroneous. Like Humpty Dumpty we are fragmented (or seem to be), but unlike him the forces of the King can put us back together. We need only cooperate and apply. Again, none of this is philosophical but eminently practical. Those who do not know the way to reintegration assume it is impossible, but those who learn the way and apply it succeed, however others may doubt.

When you make the male and the female one and the same, so that the male not be male nor the female female. Brill translates this: "When you make the male and the female into a single one, that the male be not male and the female female." And Brown: "If you establish the male with the female as a single unity so that the man will not be masculine and the woman not be feminine."

This has two basic meanings. First, we must become like the angels, transcending the condition of "man" and "woman." When Sri Ramakrishna said that the entire world was caught in the net of "woman and gold" he was speaking to men. But when speaking to women he said "man and gold." That is, to think that we are one thing and someone else another, is a delusion. We are not bodies, the seat of "gender," but spirits without body, without form. At no time are we male or female, however our present costume may be put together as we muddle through the drama of one more life on the revolving stage of this world.

Plants, insects, animals and unevolved human beings "must have their mate," but it is not so with those who have set their sights on God-realization. "And Jesus answering said unto them, The children of this world marry, and are given in marriage: but they which shall be accounted worthy to obtain that world, and the resurrection from the dead, neither marry, nor are given in marriage: neither can they die any more: for they are equal unto the angels; and are the children of God, being the children of the resurrection" (Luke 20:34-36). It is no surprise that I have never heard a sermon or read a commentary on these words. They are true, nevertheless. Male-female interaction must be abandoned by those who seek union with God. The deluded and the enslaved may not like what I am writing, but it is not written for them.

The second meaning is that the polarities of positive (male) and negative (female) within our own makeup must be transcended, and we must move beyond that duality as well, because it ties us into constant rebirth. No matter how religious or spiritual we think we are, until the state of unity is gained we will keep circling on the wheel of birth and death—even in the higher worlds beyond this one. Taoism speaks of how we sometimes act "feminine" and sometimes "masculine" according to the situation and our personal conditionings. There is even a skillful way of doing so—but only while living in duality. Before we can enter unity that dualism must be erased permanently. Otherwise we get what I heard Ma Anandamayi call (in English) "a roundtrip ticket" when she spoke to two university students about the wisdom of avoiding marriage and taking up the monastic life.

When you fashion eyes in the place of an eye, and a hand in place of a hand, and a foot in place of a foot, and a likeness in place of a likeness; then will you enter the kingdom. Brill: "When you make eyes in the place of an eye, and a hand in place of a hand, and a foot in place of a foot, an image in place of an image, then shall you enter [the kingdom]."

This either means supplying what is lacking in our inner and outer being and makeup, or replacing what is defective or deficient with better, spiritual faculties and powers, becoming no longer "flesh" but spirit. This is reflected in the ordination prayers of the Byzantine Orthodox Church in which the bishop says: "The grace divine, which always healeth that which is infirm, and completeth (supplieth) that which is wanting, elevateth through the laying-on of hands" him who is thus ordained. So Jesus is saying that we will enter the kingdom when we have the power to renew or supply that which we need for entry into Christhood and "put on the new man, which is renewed in knowledge after the image of him that created him" (Colossians 3:10; see II Corinthians 4:16 and Ephesians 4:23). As Saint Paul further said: "Be ye transformed by the renewing of your mind [nous or buddhi], that ye may prove what is that good, and acceptable, and perfect, will of God" (Romans 12:2).

The word *anakainoo* means to bring to maturity and thus make new; to impart new strength and capacity; to be changed from one mode of life (consciousness) to another. It is a total re-creation. The most significant thing about this is that Jesus says we are to effect the renewal-recreation ourselves. Otherwise the kingdom will remained closed to us.

This is a call to a higher life which is undreamed of by most religions. But that does not hinder Christ from calling us toward it.

Unity of Vision

Jesus said, I shall choose you, one out of a thousand, and two out of ten thousand, and they shall stand as a single one. (23)

Brown: "They shall stand as a single unity." Johnson: "They shall stand in unity."

Evolved people are always much more distinctive in their personalities than others. They are never joiners, team players or herd members, but pursue their individual course at all times. Peer pressure simply means nothing to them because their true peers, like them, are so strongly individual they have no interest in influencing others or being influenced by anyone. The word *monachos*–monk–means one who is solitary or is living alone, even if he lives in a community of dozens, hundreds, or thousands. (The monastery of Saint Pachomius near Aswan numbered thirty thousand monks.)

Contradictory as it may seem, as Jesus indicates those who are chosen to follow the way of Christhood, if they preserve that aspiration and do not let it be turned in the byways of ego and the world, will always be as one with each other. They will live together in harmony and cooperation, free from the elements that create conflict between ordinary people. Yet they will remain alone in their consciousness, intent on their interior cultivation at all times. Having a single goal they walk the path together in singleness of heart.

WHERE IS CHRIST?

His disciples said to him, Show us the place where you are, since it is necessary for us to seek it.

He said to them, Whoever has ears, let him hear. There is light within a man of light, and he lights up the whole world. If he does not shine, he is darkness. (24)

Johnson: His disciples requested: Teach us about the Place where you live, for we must seek it. He said: He who has ears let him hear. There is light in a man of light, who gives light to the world. If he does not give light, there is only Darkness.

In the Gospel of John we read: "Again the next day after John stood, and two of his disciples; and looking upon Jesus as he walked, he saith, Behold the Lamb of God! And the two disciples heard him speak, and they followed Jesus. Then Jesus turned, and saw them following, and saith unto them, What seek ye? They said unto him, Rabbi, (which is to say, being interpreted, Master,) where dwellest thou? He saith unto them, Come and see. They came and saw where he dwelt, and abode with him that day" (John 1:35-39).

Show us the place where you are, since it is necessary for us to seek it. There is a mystical sect in Bengal known as Bauls whose habit is to ask someone: "In what 'station' do you live?" What they are asking is what state of consciousness is the person's constant abode. When we are with highly advanced yogis we often realize that although they are physically present and interacting with us, yet they really are somewhere else altogether and living in a manner invisible to us. This was very much true of Swami Venkateshananda, a disciple of Swami Sivananda of Rishikesh.

So the disciples want to know where Jesus really "is"—and we, too, need to know that, for we also must seek that place, that level of consciousness. This is bold aspiration, but a most necessary one. Jesus came into this terrible sea of samsara to deliver us from it by calling us to higher life. Our response must be a wholehearted seeking of our own Christhood.

Whoever has ears, let him hear. Jesus knows that there is no need speaking to those who lack the capacity to understand and follow. "Everybody welcome" is a sure sign of religion that is really a business. There is no place in the kingdom of heaven for spiritual window-shoppers.

There is light within a man of light, and he lights up the whole world. He does this in two ways, inner and outer. Inwardly he lights up his own perceptions, knowing both himself and all that surrounds him through the light of his perfected consciousness (buddhi). Outwardly he illumines those in the world who have eyes to see. Just seeing him can cause a person to begin consciously seeking God. In my early sadhana days my spiritual batteries often started to go flat. Realizing that this was a dangerous condition, I would get an appointment to see Sri Daya Mata, the president of Self-Realization Fellowship. The moment she crossed the threshold of the room I would be aflame with the desire to know God. Not a word need be said. Away I would go with a full spiritual charge. Many people can give inspiring talks and even work miracles, but rare are those that can awaken us by their very sight.

If he does not shine, he is darkness. In other words, however great his reputation may be, however great the claims made by his followers, if he does not "shine" into our inmost hearts and bring us closer to God, he is nothing but darkness. I met a lot of "gurus" in India and America that had a big staff to promote them through a stream of books, photos, recordings and whatnot, but they were lumps of coal. Yet I also met simple-appearing, unassuming people whose initial glimpse thrilled my soul and I knew they were God's light in this world. I never even learned the name of some of them. They came, they shone, and they went leaving my heart aglow. This is not poetic exaggeration. In my memory I have a gallery of blessed visages to which I can put no name, but they are living in me at this moment. I also met many whose name I did learn and whose greatness is as present to me as then.

LOVE AND PROTECT

Jesus said, Love your brother like your soul, guard him like the pupil of your eye. (25)

The basis of this verse is the fundamental truth of the absolute unity and identity of all things. We are one with all that exists as well as with the Ground of Being from which all things have emanated and into which all shall return; and we are also one with all the individual spirit-consciousnesses which live eternally in that Ground of Being we usually call God.

Love

Since all are one, if we aspire to love any one thing or person we must necessarily cultivate the ability to love all, for the individual cannot be separated from the All. The plain fact is, all that exists is our "brother" who is also our "soul," for although that "brother" is not us, his/its essential being is our essential being: God. The following is the description by Saint Ambrose of Optina (Russia) of the experience that triggered his spiritual quest.

"Suddenly, I am outside of the forest, somewhere far away, in another world, quite unknown to me, never seen by me, never imagined by me.

Around me there is bright, white light! Its transcendence is so pure and enticing that I am submerged, along with my perception, into limitless depths and cannot satisfy myself with my admiration for this realm, cannot completely fill myself with its lofty spirituality. Everything is so full of beauty all around. So endearing this life–so endless the way. I am being swept across this limitless, clear space. My sight is directed upwards, does not descend anymore, does not see anything earthly. The whole of the heavenly firmament has transformed itself before me into one general bright light, pleasing to the sight.

"But I do not see the sun. I can see only its endless shining and bright light. The whole space in which I glide without hindrance, without end, without fatigue, is filled with white light, just as is its light and beautiful beings, transparent as a ray of the sun. And through them I am admiring this limitless world. The images of all these beings unknown to me are infinitely diverse and full of beauty

"I also am white and bright as they are. Over me, as over them, there reigns eternal rest. Not a single thought of mine is any longer enticed by anything earthly, not a single beat of my heart is any longer moving with human cares or earthly passion. I am all peace and rapture. But I am still moving in this infinite light, which surrounds me without change. There is nothing else in the world except for the white, bright light and these equally radiant numberless beings. But all these beings do not resemble me, nor are similar to each other; they are all endlessly varied and compellingly attractive. Amidst them, I feel myself incredibly peaceful. They evoke in me neither fear, nor amazement, nor trepidation. All that we see here does not agitate us, does not amaze us. All of us here are as if we have belonged to each other for a long time, are used to each other and are not strangers at all. We do not ask questions, we do not speak to each other about anything. We all feel and understand that there is nothing novel for us here. All our questions are solved with one glance, which sees everything and everyone. There is no trace of the wars of passions in anyone. All move in different directions, opposite to each other, not feeling any limitation, any inequality, or envy, or sorrow, or sadness. One peace reigns in all the images of entities. One light is endless for all. Oneness of life is comprehensible to all.

"My rapture at all this superseded everything. I sank into this eternal rest. No longer was my spirit disturbed by anything. And I knew nothing else earthly. None of the tribulations of my heart came to mind, even for a minute. It seemed that everything that I had experienced before on earth never existed. Such was my feeling in this new radiant world of mine. And I was at peace and joyful and desired nothing better for myself. All my earthly thoughts concerning fleeting happiness in the world died in this beautiful life, new to me, and did not come back to life again. So it seemed to me at least, there, in that better world.

"But how I came back here–I do not recall. What transitory state it was, I do not know. I only felt that I was alive, but I did not remember the world in which I lived before on earth. This did not seem at all to be a dream. Actually, about earthly things I no longer had the least notion. I only felt that the present life is mine, and that I was not a stranger in it. In this state of spirit I forgot myself and immersed myself in this light-bearing eternity. And this timelessness lasted without end, without measure, without expectation, without sleep, in this eternal rest. Thus it seemed to me that there would not be any kind of change."

This is the basis for real love.

Protect

Since the life of our "brother" is our life, it must be protected, fostered and cared for as the pupil of our eye, without which we would be blind. Those who are blind to their fellow-beings are blind to all reality, however involved they may be in their egoic delusions they think are life. Our life is the life in all beings. We are both the One and the Many, and while passing through this world we must endeavor to live every moment with that consciousness. By so doing we are preparing ourselves for that passage from multiplicity to unity that is the essence of Liberation.

It is not enough to accept the principles of essential Unity, we must demonstrate them in our own consciousness and life. That alone can lead to freedom in the infinite Spirit.

SEEING

Jesus said, You see the mote in your brother's eye, but you do not see the beam in your own eye. When you cast the beam out of your own eye, then you will see clearly to cast the mote from your brother's eye. (26)

We often want spiritual life presented to us in broad outline and generalities, but the very nature of spiritual life prevents that because spiritual life is all-encompassing and therefore includes all the details. It is very necessary to examine all the aspects of self-evolution—for that is what spiritual life really is.

Here Jesus is pointing out the inconsistent nature of a mind that is itself defective: the tiniest things are clearly seen and immense things are invisible. It is like the serial killer in Vienna who after his arrest was asked how it was he had killed a serving-maid in a great mansion whose owners were away traveling, yet had put a large supply of water and seed in a bird's cage in the house. Immediately the murderer became very indignant and shouted: "What kind of a person do you think I am that I would let a little bird starve?" It is often seen that the same people who have scruples about the smallest things will be indifferent to glaring evils in their lives. Oftentimes an exaggerated morality will be a cover or compensation for utter moral depravity, but in this case it is a matter of seeing things through the wrong end of the telescope altogether.

Several nurses who worked in mental institutions told me that there are seriously mentally ill persons, especially paranoid schizophrenics, who are totally out of touch with their personal reality but who can see other people's situations perfectly clearly and give insightful advice. Every one of the nurses admitted that on occasion they asked the mental patients to help them with personal problems, especially family difficulties, and their advice always cleared up the trouble. (The motion picture *They Might Be Giants* is all about this kind of situation.)

Usually the mote-beam exhortation of Jesus is taken to be nothing more than a rebuke of hypocrisy, but it is much more. For Jesus assures us that "then you will see clearly to cast the mote from your brother's eye," thus implying that we will gain the ability to see others' defects clearly and assist them in correcting them. This is often the work of saints: they reveal the real nature of our problems and tell us what to do about it to correct ourselves.

So this verse is a call to self-honesty and the helping of others as well.

THE FASTING AND
SABBATH OF THE SPIRIT

**Jesus said, If you do not fast as regards the world, you will
not find the kingdom. If you do not observe the Sabbath as a
Sabbath, you will not see the father. (27)**

If you do not fast as regards the world, you will not find the kingdom.
Nancy Johnson renders this: "Unless you abstain from the world,
you will not find the kingdom." The world is outside, the kingdom
is inside; our various levels or bodies are outside but our true Self,
the spirit, is inside. Therefore it only follows that the more we are
involved in the world the less we will know and live in the spirit. "For
the fashion [*schema*: order] of this world passeth away" (I Corinthians
7:3). "For all that is in the world, the lust of the flesh, and the lust of
the eyes, and the pride of life, is not of the Father, but is of the world.
And the world passeth away, and the lust thereof: but he that doeth
the will of God abideth for ever" (I John 2:16-17). Since the world
passes away, but spirit alone remains forever, the choice between the
world and the spirit should be easy, but few make the right choice. It
takes many lives for us to get the idea.

One of Yogananda's disciples moved to a new house that had an alley running behind it where people put out their garbage for collection on Fridays. The first Friday he was there, he saw his dog in the neighbor's garbage. He went to investigate and found the dog greedily eating a huge amount of bacon grease. (In those days it was common for people to drain off meat grease in a container and then discard it in the garbage.) The dog ate all the grease and spent the entire weekend sick with dry heaves–a distressful and painful result. But the next week the dog ate the bacon grease again, and again spent the weekend sick. This happened for a total of twenty-three weeks before the dog quit eating the grease. His owner would tell this to people and laugh and say: "This world is nothing but 'bacon grease,' and people have no more sense than my dog. From life to life they keep eating the 'grease' and getting sick." Then looking pointedly at them he would ask: "And when are *you* going to quit the bacon grease?"

If you do not observe the Sabbath as a Sabbath, you will not see the father. Saint Paul wrote: "There remaineth therefore a rest to the people of God. For he that is entered into his rest, he also hath ceased from his own works, as God did from his. Let us labour therefore to enter into that rest" (Hebrews 4:9-11). The word rather oddly translated "rest" is actually *Sabbatismos*–Sabbath–which means the seventh day.

Every human being has seven levels of consciousness which correspond to the seven chakras of the yoga system. These levels are symbolized in various ways in the Bible: the seven days of creation, the seven days of holy week, the seven "churches" and the seven "seals" of Revelation. The opening of these seals in Revelation represents the opening of the different levels of consciousness from the lowest to the highest, from the first to the seventh. Saint John tells us about the opening of the seals. The first six produced a great deal of cataclysmic phenomena, but "when he had opened the seventh seal, there was silence in heaven" (Revelation 8:1). The evolutionary journey was completed and the yogi entered into the sabbath-rest of silence. As Buddha said: "Birth is exhausted [that is, the karma that produces birth is dissolved, has ceased to exist], the holy life has been lived out, what can be done is done, of this there is no more beyond." Perfection having been reentered, nothing remains to be done or not done. This was understood even in the Old Testament: "The Lord is in his holy temple: let all the earth keep silence before him" (Habakkuk 2:20). "Be silent, O all flesh, before the Lord: for he is raised up out of his holy habitation" (Zechariah 2:13).

The transcendent Father dwells in the seventh level of cosmic existence, beyond all else. The Son and the Holy Spirit manifest and evolve the other six levels that lead to the seventh. To know God we must ascend to that. Those who do so shall see the Father with the single eye of perfect enlightenment (Matthew 6:22).

HOW JESUS SAW
THE WORLD

Jesus said, I took my place in the midst of the world, and I appeared to them in flesh. I found all of them intoxicated; I found none of them thirsty. And my soul became afflicted for the sons of men, because they are blind in their hearts and do not have sight; for empty they came into the world, and empty too they seek to leave the world. But for the moment they are intoxicated. When they shake off their wine, then they will repent. (28)

I took my place in the midst of the world, and I appeared to them in flesh. This sentence is important because it shows that the Gospel of Thomas is not a Gnostic text in the usual sense, because the Gnostics denied that Jesus had a real, physical body, and claimed that his body was only an appearance, a mirage. Here Jesus says: "I appeared to them *in flesh.*"

It is also important because it tells us that Jesus took on a fully human body which was capable of all the distracting (and addicting) pain and pleasure common to human bodies, that he was right down here in the material world with us. In this way he proved that we need not be "subject to the flesh," as is often claimed, but can make it subject to our spiritualized consciousness as did he. He, like all yogis, demonstrated that the body is an instrument of enlightenment when used in the way it was intended. Only the yogi has a chance of being normal, or even human, in the true sense. Without yoga there is not only no hope, there is no potential.

I found all of them intoxicated. Here is the plight of humanity. We are inwardly poisoned–the literal meaning of intoxicated–by drinking in the world through our senses and considering it the sole reality and the standard of thought and behavior. "Eat, drink, and be merry for tomorrow we die" is the kind of thinking produced, along with the contradictory illusion that we will never die, that death need not occupy a single thought in our mind. We are drunkards, out of our minds and stumbling through life aimlessly. Drunks think they are very clever and happy, whatever mess they are in. Drunkenness is worse than death because it is delusion. And the suffering of the drunk is terrible, however much it is denied or ignored. "All we like sheep have gone astray" (Isaiah 53:6), whatever might be claimed to the contrary. Drunks often accuse others of being drunk while insisting they are not. A lot of people are the same who are drunk on the world and its follies.

I found none of them thirsty. This is the horrible part of it: drunk on the world, no one has a genuine spiritual thirst. However miserable they may be, their thoughts never turn to the higher things that will remove their pain. This is becoming increasingly worse as the years go by. For example, the Titanic was a kind of pleasure palace for the wealthy who drowned themselves in distractions long before being drowned in the ocean. Yet, when the boat was sinking the string quartet that had been entertaining them before began to play "Nearer My God To Thee" until the very end. The doomed people prayed to God and at least in their last moments thought of their immortal souls and eternal verities. Better late then never, truly. But today it is a very different matter. I cannot count the number of near-death experiences I have been told, and not one person thought of God or the world beyond this one. Many say they thought about their families, and one friend of mine who nearly drowned off the coast of California, having gone for a night swim, told me: "They say when you are going down for the last time your whole life flashes before your eyes, but all I did was think: 'You old fool, what are people going to think about the way you died?'" A priest I know of saw his plane going toward what seemed an unavoidable collision with another plane. "What a hell of a way to go," was his "last" thought.

Corny as it may seem, Roy Acuff's famous song *Wreck on the Highway* says it well:

Who did you say it was, brother?
Who was it fell by the way?
When whiskey and blood ran together,
Did you hear anyone pray?

When I heard the crash on the highway
I knew what it was from the start.
I went to the scene of destruction
And a picture was stamped on my heart.

There was whiskey and blood all together
Mixed with glass where they lay.
Death played her hand in destruction
But I didn't hear nobody pray.

I wish I could change this sad story
That I am now telling you,
But there is no way I can change it,
For somebody's life is now through.

Their soul has been called by the Master.
They died in a crash on the way.
And I heard the groans of the dying.
But I didn't hear nobody pray.

I didn't hear nobody pray, dear brother,
I didn't hear nobody pray.
I heard the crash on the highway
But I didn't hear nobody pray.

If you prefer a more literary form, then here is how Vachel Lindsay said it in his poem "The Leaden-Eyed."

It is the world's one crime its babes grow dull,
Its poor are ox-like, limp and leaden-eyed.
Not that they starve; but starve so dreamlessly,
Not that they sow, but that they seldom reap,
Not that they serve, but have no gods to serve,
Not that they die, but that they die like sheep.

God lamented through the prophet-poet David: "They know not, neither will they understand; they walk on in darkness: all the foundations of the earth are out of course. I have said, Ye are gods; and all of you are children of the most High. But ye shall die like men, and fall like one of the princes" (Psalms 82:5-7).

And my soul became afflicted for the sons of men, because they are blind in their hearts and do not have sight. Jesus did not sneer or despise humans when he saw their sad condition. Like Buddha, he was moved with compassion. "When he saw the multitudes, he was moved with compassion on them, because they fainted, and were scattered abroad, as sheep having no shepherd" (Matthew 9:36). He knew their hearts were blind and therefore were without true comprehension of themselves, the world, or their purpose of existence.

For empty they came into the world, and empty too they seek to leave the world. Believing either that emptiness is natural or that the things of the world can fill their emptiness, they remain empty. I well remember looking at my parents when I was three or four years old and knowing that at the end of their lives they would not have done anything, gone anywhere, learned anything, accomplished anything, or really been anything. And so it was. I loved them, but I saw clearly the emptiness, and it make me resolve to not be the same. Decades later I went back and visited my family. I clearly saw that spiritually speaking they were just sitting in their graves waiting to die, and even death would make no difference. The next life would be just another nondescript boxcar in the train of their lives. Eventually, of course, it will change. But not now.

But for the moment they are intoxicated. When they shake off their wine, then they will repent. We are eternal and divine in nature, however hidden that fact may be from ourselves and those around us. Consequently, the intoxication will not last forever. The poisoned wine of materiality will be pushed away and all will change the direction of their present lives and future births, either here or in higher worlds. Patterson and Maeyer do not translate the second half of this sentence: "they will repent," but rather: "they will change their ways." As Jesus said: "Because I live, ye shall live also" (John 14:19). When we walk the same path he walked, then "like as Christ was raised up from the dead by the glory of the Father, even so we also should walk in newness of life" (Romans 6:4), resurrected with him into God for ever.

HIDDEN TREASURE

Jesus said, If the flesh came into being because of spirit, it
is a wonder. But if spirit came into being because of the body,
it is a wonder of wonders. Indeed, I am amazed at how this
great wealth has made its home ["come to dwell"–Patterson
and Maeyer] in this poverty. (29)

Swami Vivekananda pointed out that one of the vast differences
between East and West is the East's understanding that Spirit is
the source of matter, that matter is the expression of consciousness–in
contrast to the "science" of the West's idea that consciousness (spirit)
evolves out of matter and therefore is the expression of matter. Jesus
is being satirical in saying: "if spirit came into being because of the
body, it is a wonder of wonders." It is very like the statement of George
Bernard Shaw: "In the Roman Catholic Church a great miracle takes
place: bread and wine become the body and blood of Jesus Christ. But
in the Church of England an even greater miracle occurs: bread and
wine become the body and blood of Jesus Christ, and at the same time
they do not become the body and blood of Jesus Christ!" It is indeed
a wonder that infinite Spirit, "this great wealth," has sent forth from
Its own being the universes and all sentient beings that inhabit them.

The Mundaka Upanishad says it perfectly: "As the web comes out of the spider and is withdrawn, as plants grow from the soil and hair from the body of man, so springs the universe from the eternal Brahman.

"Brahman willed that it should be so, and brought forth out of himself the material cause of the universe; from this came the primal energy, and from the primal energy mind, from mind the subtle elements, from the subtle elements the many worlds, and from the acts performed by beings in the many worlds the chain of cause and effect—the reward and punishment of works.

"Brahman sees all, knows all; he is knowledge itself. Of him are born cosmic intelligence, name, form, and the material cause of all created beings and things" (Mundaka Upanishad 1.1.7-9).

This demonstrates very well that a priest of the Saint Thomas Christian (Malankara Orthodox) Church of India spoke the simple truth when he told me: "You cannot understand the teachings of Jesus if you do not know the scriptures of India."

ONE

Jesus said, Where there are three gods, they are gods. Where
there are two or one, I am with him. (30)
> *Patterson and Maeyer:* "Jesus said, "Where there are three deities,
> they are divine. Where there are two or one, I am with that one."

It would be dishonest to say that I believe I know what this means. I
can, however, speculate. "Where there are three deities, they are divine,"
may mean that a person is what he is at any point in evolutionary time.
However, whatever the number God is with them at all times. Therefore
we are never alone–there are always two, at least.

God is the prevailing and ever-present factor in the life of all sentient
beings. Consequently, this all-pervading Presence should be the focus
of our lives, because It is the Life-principle itself, and the force behind
our entry into, and our exit from, relative existence. Eventually we will
discover that It is not just the basis of our existence, It is the Totality
of all existence, that when there are "two" there is still only One(ness).
When God says that beside him there is no other, he means it in the
sense of absolute Oneness–divine Unity. This is the truth we must realize
if we would be liberated from the attendant confusion and pain of the
illusion of duality.

The Power of Unbelief

Jesus said, No prophet is accepted in his own village; no physician heals those who know him. (31)

For the last forty years I never read or hear these words without thinking of Anand Maharaj, an outstanding yogi I became friends with in northern India. Anand Maharaj was unique among the yogis of my acquaintance. He was insistent upon living in the most simple manner, and was the most unassuming person I have ever met. Although possessed of vast yogic knowledge and power, he kept it completely hidden. Only those of equal development, or those to whom he gave a glimpse of his real stature, had any idea of his inner attainment.

He told me that he had left home to be a yogi when he was only twelve years old. For some time he wandered around India, sometimes staying in a place a few weeks or so. Because he was obviously a spiritual prodigy, he was shown great respect and even love. This was pleasant, but he realized this it was also a terrible danger, for in such circumstances the yogi can end up admiring and loving his ego. He said that he pondered a long time over this dilemma and finally decided that the wise thing would be to return to his home village and live in the forest outside it.

He did so, and his surmise was right. Everyone, including his family, sneered at him calling him lazy, a fool and a fraud. Having no money or possessions, he begged for his food as monks have done for thousands of years in India. No one would give him anything, but he resolved that he would not leave even if he starved. Eventually the people grudgingly began to give him scraps to eat, and things continued in this way until he became an adult. When he felt that he had learned the lessons of humility and detachment he left that place. Then, with the perversity of human nature, representatives of the village came and begged him to return, even promising to build him an ashram. Since this was exactly what he did not want, he refused and vowed never to return. When I met him some decades later he was still keeping to his resolution of total simplicity of life and renunciation.

The meaning of this verse is somewhat filled out by the following from the Gospel of Saint Matthew: "Jesus said unto them, A prophet is not without honour, save in his own country, and in his own house. And he did not many mighty works there because of their unbelief" (Matthew 13:57-58).

We do control our life, however weak and directionless we may think we are. Such a belief about ourselves makes it so, practically speaking, and it is true about others and their influence in our lives. Over and over again in history we find accounts of people who attain greatness and the admiration of all, but their families and those who knew them earlier refused to honor them and claimed they were still what they were perviously. Parents continually reduce their offspring to childhood, not matter how successful they might be. I knew a man in his sixties whose mother treated him like he was five years old, and the moment he walked in the house he reverted to five-year-old behavior. I have known gifted people who just could not show their abilities before their parents or families, but became mentally and emotionally paralyzed. Many great musicians have not been able to perform if they knew their parents or families were in the audience.

The rejective attitudes of those close to us can bring us to a halt. This is the negative side of mind power.

When people asked Anandamayi Ma: "What are you?" she would reply: "I am whatever you think I am." Yogananda records a similar statement in *Autobiography of a Yogi*:

"A woman chela once asked the guru [Lahiri Mahasaya] for his photograph. He handed her a print, remarking, 'If you deem it a protection, then it is so; otherwise it is only a picture.'

"A few days later this woman and Lahiri Mahasaya's daughter-in-law happened to be studying the Bhagavad Gita at a table behind which hung the guru's photograph. An electrical storm broke out with great fury.

"'Lahiri Mahasaya, protect us!' The women bowed before the picture. Lightning struck the book which they had been reading, but the two devotees were unhurt.

"'I felt as though a sheet of ice had been placed around me to ward off the scorching heat,' the chela explained."

Because readers might not understand, Yogananda did not exactly relay the words of Lahiri Mahasaya regarding his photograph. He actually said: "If you think it is God [Bhagavan], then it is God." And it proved to be so, for he was God in human form.

"According to your faith be it unto you" said Jesus (Matthew 9:29); and it is the same with unbelief and denial: nothing will happen. It is our choice.

SPIRITUAL STRENGTH

Jesus said, A city being built on a high mountain and fortified cannot fall, nor can it be hidden. (32)

Each of us is a city according to various spiritual traditions, so we can apply this verse to ourselves.

If we would be successful as human beings, we must build our city–establish ourselves–on the heights of spiritual aspiration, inspiration, and realization. Elevation of consciousness is the only way to do this, not through abstract theorizing and endless word-gaming. Spiritual practice is the way of constructing our life as a city of God.

This city must be protected from the dangers of this world and the forces of ignorance, material and metaphysical. Therefore it must be walled about by the scrupulous practice of discipline and right conduct. This will result in a strength and stability that cannot shaken. One of the best means for this is the Eightfold Path expounded by the Buddha:

1. Right view
2. Right intention
3. Right speech
4. Right action

5. Right livelihood
6. Right effort
7. Right mindfulness
8. Right meditation

The material world is preceded by the spiritual world; in fact the material world is an extension of the spiritual world. It is necessary, then, that spiritual development and evolution should result in the development and evolution of the outer life. It cannot be hidden if it is real. That is why when a Brahmin met Buddha right after his enlightenment, he was struck with awe at his very appearance. The entire outer life is changed when the inner life is changed. It is inescapable.

SPEAK IT OUT

Jesus said, Preach from your housetops that which you will hear in your ear. For no one lights a lamp and puts it under a bushel, nor does he put it in a hidden place, but rather he sets it on a lampstand so that everyone who enters and leaves will see its light. (33)

This is a continuation of the theme of the preceding verse, but it is dealing with the manifestation of inner realization in relation to others. First a person must attain insight, and then he must express it. Although he should not be annoying people like a bullying missionary, at every moment going on and on about his ideas to those who are not interested, his actions should proclaim his spiritual vision, and so should his dealing with others and his conversation as well. For example, we should not hide our dedication to spiritual life, but make it clear by our firmness in the observation of right conduct. When asked to betray our principles we should never be harsh or accusatory, but we must be firm in our refusal to do so.

People are stumbling through this world in varying degrees of blindness. We are obligated to help them with calm and wise words. When we understand their situation we should diplomatically give our insight.

One time a man lamented to Yogananda that his son was going to hell because he got drunk. So Yogananda suggested that the next time his son got drunk he should make a huge bonfire and throw him in it! When the man expressed disgust at Yogananda's words, the Master asked him how it was that he thought that God, who was also the boy's loving father, would throw him into the fires of hell.

Being ashamed of our religious principles and practice is not just bad for us, it robs others of a chance to learn of a better way of doing things. For example, we frequent a restaurant that is highly recommended by members of some spiritual groups, and their members are usually to be found there. Yet we have never seen a single one either pray before eating or bless their food. No one would laugh or object, least of all the owner who is a devout Buddhist and has many images of Buddha displayed in the restaurant.

Even more to the point, when people tell us of their problems we should sympathize and promise to pray for them, and explain the spiritual perspective on their troubles. Otherwise, how will we fulfill Saint Paul's injunction to be lights in the world (Philippians 2:15)?

THE BLIND

Jesus said, If a blind man leads a blind man, they will both fall into a pit. (34)

Nancy Johnson: "When the blind lead the blind, they fall together into the ditch."

Everyone in this world needs instruction, from the infant that has to be taught to feed itself and to talk and walk, to those that would scale the heights in any field of knowledge or action. Even the simplest thing requires learning and practice in some form. At the same time we are all called upon to lead others into the same knowing that we possess. This being so, we must be careful in choosing a teacher and in deciding if we ourselves are truly qualified to teach others.

If we follow an ignorant person we will go into greater ignorance. As Jesus said: "If the light that is in thee be darkness, how great is that darkness!" (Matthew 6:23). Conversely, if we being ignorant presume to teach another we will lead them into increased darkness. It is better to know nothing and be aware of it than to mistakenly think we know something. For example, my paternal grandfather had bought a driving license at a drug store, ordered a car from a catalog, and learned to drive by reading the booklet that came along with the car when it was delivered.

After a time he decided that my grandmother should learn to drive also. So out they went and came back with the two of them quite satisfied that she could drive as well as he did. But when the whole family went out one day and he had her drive, he was amazed to see her gripping the steering wheel and moving it back and forth in tiny, quick jerks. "What are you doing?" he demanded, and she told him: "I am giving it more gas!" Something had been missed.

You may not believe it (I hardly do myself, in retrospect), but I had a hymnbook that included a song entitled "The Automobile of Life." Silly as the symbolism may be, the basic idea is true, and we should learn from my grandparents' experience and be very sure that we only follow those that can see, and lead only those that can see, while being very sure that we ourselves can see.

THE SECRET OF
SPIRITUAL SECURITY

**Jesus said, It is not possible for anyone to enter the house
of a strong man and take it by force unless he binds his hands;
then he will (be able to) ransack his house. (35)**

Jesus is not giving us instructions on how to be a thief, he is telling
us how to not be overcome and looted spiritually. Of course, it is all
symbolic of the way the spirit which dwells in the house of the body
becomes rendered helpless and despoiled.

Many are the thieves that lurk about seeking to steal our spiritual and
mental property. In Revelation Jesus says to us: "Hold that fast which thou
hast, that no man take thy crown" (Revelation 3:11). Our crown is our
spiritual destiny which the Beloved Disciple outlined, saying: "Beloved,
now are we the sons of God, and it doth not yet appear what we shall be:
but we know that, when he shall appear, we shall be like him; for we shall
see him as he is" (I John 3:2). And Saint Paul: "The mystery which hath
been hid from ages and from generations, now is made manifest to his
saints: to whom God would make known what is the riches of the glory
of this mystery among the Gentiles; which is Christ in you, the hope of

glory" (Colossians 1:26, 27). The revelation of our inner Christ is our crown which we must guard diligently against losing to thieves.

And who are these thieves? Anything which hinders or erodes our spiritual progress. There are a lot of them, which is why we have to be so vigilant against their incursion into the house of our mind and heart. The hands that bind are the inhibition of our spiritual powers and the knowledge of their use, for they are the tools of our self-evolution. Once we lose our spiritual insight and empowerment, we shall become enslaved and ruthlessly pillaged by the thieves we let into our house through neglect and carelessness. The result is often–if not usually–spiritual death.

This is no idle fancy or exaggeration. Throughout my life I have seen people who were doing well and progressing spiritually suddenly fall and become totally ruined in body, mind and spirit. Very few ever recovered from it. I have known people that radiated goodness and purity, whose love and dedication for God were unquestioned. And I have seen them struck down by even small things that they were not on their guard to resist. Their hands were bound and they lost the life of the spirit through that bondage. Their grief and misery pervaded the rest of their lives. One or two escaped from the swamp, but remained crippled for the rest of their life, dim in consciousness, mechanical and rote in their religious life.

So we must make our hands strong and skilled and be on our guard at all times. As Saint Paul further said: "Therefore we ought to give the more earnest heed to the things which we have heard, lest at any time we should let them slip" (Hebrews 2:1). *Pararrueo* means to slip from our grasp the way water taken in our hand escapes our grasp. It also implies an extremely easy slipping away–again like water.

The best way to keep our spirit-hands strong is simple: constant use through always pushing onward to new spiritual territory, never letting them rest, but always busy in the real work, the "one thing needful" (Luke 10:38-42). If we do so, then Jesus guarantees that we shall have "treasure in the heavens that faileth not, where no thief approacheth" (Luke 12:33).

LIVE CAREFREE

**Jesus said, Do not be concerned from morning until evening
and from evening until morning about what you will wear. (36)**

Although Jesus uses the example of clothing, the principle of these
words apply to every external factor in our life. The idea is simple:
at no time should we be worried or fearful about any aspect of our
outer life. Certainly, we should give careful and intelligent thought to
our necessities, for God does not drop everything we need down from
heaven the way a bird feeds its young, who only need to open their
mouths and make a racket to get their parent's attention.

The basis for Jesus' exhortation is the fact that God is aware of every
atom of our life, and has so arranged the universe and the laws of action
and reaction (karma) that everything will work in harmony and for our
betterment. Even if momentarily things seemingly are not going well,
that is our short-sighted evaluation. But in the long run we will see that
only good is occurring in our life.

Unashamed Before God

His disciples said, When will you become revealed to us and when shall we see you? Jesus said, When you disrobe without being ashamed

> [*Nancy Johnson:* "When you shed your shame."] and take up your garments and place them under your feet like little children and tread on them, then will you see the son of the living one, and you will not be afraid. (37)

Adam, Eve and Isaiah

In paradise Adam and Eve "were both naked… and were not ashamed" (Genesis 2:5) because of their consciousness of spirit rather than of the body. But through their misdeeds "the eyes of them both were opened, and they knew that they were naked" (Genesis 3:7). So we see that shame and fear come from moral transgression and its attendant guilt.

In the book of Isaiah, we are told that God told the prophet: "Go and loose the sackcloth from off thy loins, and put off thy shoe from thy foot. And he did so, walking naked and barefoot" (Isaiah 20:2 3). A person who converses with God is not likely to care about the opinion of mortals.

Sri Ramakrishna

On Sri Ramakrishna's birthday in 1883, he remarked to a few of his disciples: "One cannot be spiritual as long as one has shame or fear. Great will be the joy today. But those fools who will not sing or dance, mad with God's name, will never attain God." In the devotional scriptures of India shame and fear are considered two of the eight fetters of delusion which prevent someone from attaining spiritual realization. Therefore Sri Ramakrishna counseled a devotee, Sri Vijay Krishna Goswami: "Surrender yourself completely to God, and set aside all such things as fear and shame." In this verse we see that nearly two thousand years before, Jesus who had gained his wisdom in India taught the very same thing.

Sri Ramakrishna also said that a person of high consciousness, established in non-duality, may act like a child, forgetting all about clothing and walking naked, unaware of the fact. "The Master showed his devotees the manners and movements of a paramahamsa: the gait of a child, face beaming with laughter, eyes swimming in joy, and body completely naked." And he said: "A child is beyond all ideas of purity and impurity. He is not bound by social conventions. He doesn't hesitate to come out naked before others."

Krishna

Long, long before either Jesus or Sri Ramakrishna, the same principle was taught by Krishna. In ancient India there was a special season when young girls engaged in various spiritual observances to ensure that they would marry an ideal husband. Once the young female devotees of Krishna, the gopis, practiced those disciplines to gain Krishna as their husband. When they were bathing in the Jumna river, Krishna stole their clothing and sat up in a tree watching them. When the gopis started coming out of the water and caught sight of Krishna, they ran back in and stood with the water up to their necks so he would not see them naked. Indignantly they demanded their clothes, and Krishna told them that the only way they could have them was to come out of the water, go over to him, and take the clothes from his hand. They fussed for quite a while, but eventually all did so. The lesson was twofold: 1) love cancels all shame, and 2) the soul cannot come to God and be wedded to him unless it comes naked, divested of all that is not spirit. To return to our Source we must lay aside all that we have acquired by entering into relative, evolutionary existence. Otherwise the aspiration is mere emotion, not based on intelligent will.

Saint John Maximovitch

Here is a twentieth-century example known to me personally. I was privileged to meet the modern Russian Orthodox saint, Saint John Maximovitch, the bishop of San Francisco. I also had the good fortune to meet Bishop Sava of Edmonton, Canada, who was a very close friend of Saint John. He said that one time he was walking with Saint John down a street in Manhattan. Saint John was wearing a silk cassock that a Chinese laywoman had made for him. When Bishop Sava remarked that it was an extremely nice-looking garment, Saint John stopped walking, said: "You may have it," and began pulling it off right there on the street. This was shocking enough to Bishop Sava, but he immediately saw that Saint John was totally naked underneath the cassock! He knew that it would be useless to reason with the saint, so he turned and ran as fast as he could, away from the impending disaster. So Saint John let the cassock slip down and resumed serenely walking. Bishop Sava might have known fear and shame and acted accordingly, but obviously Saint John did not.

Peer pressure

Also inseparable from this is the necessity to not permit ourselves to be influenced by the opinion of others at any time. I have known people who either abandoned spiritual life or did not even take it up because of pressure from friends, family, or society. This is a terrible weakness, and even if we are prone to it we must steel ourselves against it and do that which is right. In spiritual matters this is an absolute must.

In Mahayana Buddhism it is said that the moment a person decides to seek higher consciousness a multitude of buddhas and bodhisattvas become aware of it and begin to help them in their quest. That is the only "peer pressure" we should seek or even acknowledge. As Saint Paul told the spiritual aspirants of his day: "Ye are no more strangers and foreigners, but fellow citizens with the saints, and of the household of God" (Ephesians 2:19).

When we live in the paradise-consciousness of the holy ones I have cited, then we, too, will be freed from shame and fear. Christ will then be revealed to us in his true nature, for we will have entered into awareness of our own spirit-nature. Seeing ourselves we will see Christ. And seeing Christ, we will see the Father (John 14:9).

AT THE SOURCE

Jesus said, Many times have you desired to hear these words which I am saying to you, and you have no one else to hear them from. There will be days when you will look for me and will not find me. (38)

Nancy Johnson: "When you have no other to listen to, days will come when you shall search, but never find me."]

Inner yearning

We all come into this world with a destiny that is known to us on the subconscious level, and which often trickles up onto the conscious level. Recently I was at a spiritual center and a man asked me how I became a monk. When I told him I had received an intuition about being a monk when I was four years old, he laughed and told me that when he was six he saw a photograph of Rocky Marciano in a stack of old newspapers and instantly knew that he was going to become a boxer–and did so very successfully. This destiny is what the Bhagavad Gita calls *swadharma*: the path each person is meant to follow to further their evolutionary development. For me it was monastic life and for him it was the boxing ring. Though seemingly poles apart, for each of us it was the same: destiny.

This being so, we often feel impulses from deep within that are messages from the higher mind pointing us to our intended future. That is why Jesus tells the disciples that previously they had desired to hear the teachings he was then giving them. Actually, the wisdom he imparted was already within them in seed form awaiting to be awakened. The highest learning is really a remembering of what we have always known but forgotten when coming into this material world. We are not convinced of truth, we recognize it. The only purpose of a true spiritual teacher or teaching is the enabling of us to open our spiritual awareness and, as Jesus said: "Every scribe which is instructed unto the kingdom of heaven is like unto a man that is an householder, which bringeth forth out of his treasure things new and old" (Matthew 13:52).

No other teacher

There is no place in spiritual life for false modesty and displays of humility that mask one of the worst forms of spiritual pride: the desire to be thought humble and without ego. Therefore Jesus tells them quite plainly that he alone can teach them that which their souls have been longing for. At the age of twelve he had proven that the spiritual authorities in Israel had nothing to teach him, and had gone to India where over the course of more than a dozen years he learned the wisdom he had returned to teach to any who would listen.

We can wander for lifetimes in confusion and dead-end byways if we do not find a teacher who can not only tell us the truth, but can show us to way to know those truths for ourselves by teaching us the way to open the inner omniscience possessed by each one of us in potential form. This inner power is the "image and likeness" of God (Genesis 1:26) that is the very nature of every sentient being. Jesus was such a teacher as were and are all the enlightened masters throughout the ages. Krishna, Buddha, Jesus and others of their status still are guiding disciples to the Light that is their true Self.

Looking in vain

We must understand and experience the real, ever-present nature and presence of those great master-teachers. Those who were used to only being with the physical embodiment of Jesus, and had not opened their own spiritual sight and become aware of his inner being along with theirs, after his departure from them looked for him in vain and lamented that they had lost the source of their needed guidance.

The same thing happened in the twentieth century with the disciples of Ramana Maharshi in India. He kept telling them through the years that they must not obsess and depend on his physical presence, but gain their own inner realization, otherwise they would be desolated at his death and be without a guide. And it happened just as he said. Fortunately some of them then got busy and found guidance and wisdom within, but others simply formed a personality cult and kept on obsessing on his past physical embodiment and blinded themselves to his abiding spiritual presence. As he had told someone: "They think I am leaving [dying], but where would I go?" He knew himself as the omnipresent Inner Reality which they also were.

Buddha said: "Only turn around and lo! the Other Shore." It is the same with the great masters. If we will turn within and call we shall surely find them, or they will send us external assistance in the form of their true disciples who are themselves progressing to equal their beloved masters.

The message is clear: the inner search is everything.

THE RELIGION OF IGNORANCE

Jesus said, The pharisees and the scribes have taken the keys of knowledge [gnosis] and hidden them. They themselves have not entered, nor have they allowed to enter those who wish to. You, however, be as wise as serpents and as innocent as doves. (39)

The pharisees and the scribes have taken the keys of knowledge [gnosis] and hidden them. Perhaps the saddest aspect of this is that they no doubt had no idea they were keys and that there even was knowledge they did not already have. Instead they no doubt thought the things they suppressed were wrong and somehow subversive to their ideas and control.

Most of the time those who suppress knowledge do so because they think it is nonsense and they are making sure no one gets confused. On the other hand, there are those who know they are hiding truth, being consciously and intentionally evil. To such, Jesus said: "Ye are of your father the devil, and the lusts of your father ye will do. He was a murderer from the beginning, and abode not in the truth, because there is no truth in him. When he speaketh a lie, he speaketh of his own: for he is a liar, and the father of it" (John 8:44).

Whatever the motives, those who seek gnosis are always portrayed by these people as enemies of God and truth. Considering themselves as the forces of right, they are are vicious toward them in both word and deed. Basically, they hide the truth beneath their lies.

They themselves have not entered, nor have they allowed to enter those who wish to. Hatred and fear are the reactions of such people toward both truth and those who seek truth. I well remember as a child seeing in our local post office a huge green, black-spattered poster with the words: BEWARE THE HOXEY CANCER CURE! That was all. A few years later a woman I knew developed an inoperable brain tumor. She went to the Hoxey Clinic in Dallas, Texas for a few weeks and returned completely free of the tumor. Fortunately, neither she nor her parents heeded the false warning actually put out by our government. During my last year in high school one of my fellow students who planned to become a nurse gave a report on the Hoxey treatment, demonstrating by medical principles that it was absolutely safe and effective.

The most rabid enemies of truth are those that themselves once subscribed to it and then sold out for some reason and became its opponents. In many instances the most hysterical enemies of truth are those that simply hate the idea of people escaping from the prison they are too weak or corrupt to abandon themselves.

You, however, be as wise as serpents and as innocent as doves. We do not blame these people, argue with them or declare them our enemies. We ignore their attempts at repression and march on in our chosen path, unashamed and unafraid. Yet we must be wise and full of good will to all that oppose us. *Satyam Eva Jayate:* Truth Alone Triumphs.

The Patterson and Maeyer translation says we are to be "simple as doves." Wisdom is noble, but cunning and machinations are base. We must avoid such absolutely. Yet we must be fearless and straightforward at the same time, diplomatic but never conciliatory. Naturally we will be denounced as crazy, evil, negative, divisive, inflexible, stubborn, bigoted and all the things that our accusers themselves really are. That is why Jesus said, "Whereunto shall I liken this generation? It is like unto children sitting in the markets, and calling unto their fellows, and saying, We have piped unto you, and ye have not danced; we have mourned unto you, and ye have not lamented" (Matthew 11:16-17). In the *Gospel of Sri Ramakrishna* we find this good advice:

"The conversation was about worldly men, who look down on those who aspire to spiritual things. The Master was talking about the great number of such people in the world, and about how to deal with them.

"MASTER (to Narendra): How do you feel about it? Worldly people say all kinds of things about the spiritually minded. But look here! When an elephant moves along the street, any number of curs and other small animals may bark and cry after it; but the elephant doesn't even look back at them. If people speak ill of you, what will you think of them?

"NARENDRA: I shall think that dogs are barking at me.

"MASTER (Smiling): Oh, no! You mustn't go that far, my child! (*Laughter*). God dwells in all beings. But you may be intimate only with good people; you must keep away from the evil-minded. God is even in the tiger; but you cannot embrace the tiger on that account. (*Laughter*). You may say, Why run away from a tiger, which is also a manifestation of God? The answer to that is: Those who tell you to run away are also manifestations of God–and why shouldn't you listen to them?"

We must hold firmly to our principles while doing all that is reasonable to "follow peace with all men" as Saint Paul counsels us (Hebrews 12:14), even those who claim we are they "that have turned the world upside down" (Acts 17:6).

"Behold, I send you forth as sheep in the midst of wolves: be ye therefore wise as serpents, and harmless as doves" (Matthew 10:16).

WITHIN GOD

Jesus said, A grapevine has been planted outside of the father, but being unsound, it will be pulled up by its roots and destroyed. (40)

Outside of the Father

Any situation, person, or object that is not planted and rooted in the awareness of God, or in the purpose to realize God, must be drastically ejected from our life. If we do not do this, its destruction will happen as a consequence of the nature of things, the problem being that we may be spiritually (and even physically) destroyed along with it.

Being in the "shadow"

This translation by Lambdin and four others give significant nuances regarding the state of being outside the providence of God.

Lambdin: "Unsound" in the sense of being defective, lacking what is necessary for growth and survival.

Patterson and Maeyer: "Not strong" and therefore weak and without stamina or health.

Nancy Johnson: "Not supported" the way a plant is by a stake. In other words, we will not have God as a support to guide and protect us and be our reservoir of strength.

Brown: "Not viable," not even legitimate, because of being contrary to the divine order and evolutionary plan. Also it cannot work or succeed.

Brill: "Not established" or rooted and made safe and secure in God.

These descriptive phrases can be applied to us and to anything not within the greater life of God. Archimandrite Sophrony Sakharov, a twentieth-century authority on mystical life in the Eastern Christian tradition, wrote a book entitled *His Life Is Mine.* That pretty well says it all. It is God's intention to live in us so we may live in him in the state of *theosis,* the state of deification. This is the condition of total unity of being, a far cry from the feeble condition popularly called "a good Christian life." This is not the state of a mere Christian, but the state of a Christ. That is the essence of Christianity, and must be our intention and eventual attainment. Otherwise in the summing up after death known as the judgment, lifetime after lifetime we will hear the words: "I know thy works, that thou art neither cold nor hot: I would thou wert cold or hot. So then because thou art lukewarm, and neither cold nor hot, I will spue thee out of my mouth" (Revelation 3:15, 16). It is not enough to be a good Christian, we must become a true Christ.

SPIRITUAL GAIN AND LOSS

Jesus said, Whoever has something in his hand will receive more, and whoever has nothing will be deprived of even the little he has. (41)

B *rill:* "He who has in his hand, to him shall be given; and he who has not, from him shall be taken even the little that he has."

The Gospel of Matthew has: "Whosoever hath, to him shall be given, and he shall have more abundance: but whosoever hath not, from him shall be taken away even that he hath" (13:12). And: "Unto every one that hath shall be given, and he shall have abundance: but from him that hath not shall be taken away even that which he hath" (25:29; see verses 14-30 for a parable on this).

This verse presents a vital spiritual principle, one which everyone ought to know, but which few really do. Spiritual and material life often parallel one another. There are spiritual assets just as there are material assets, and laws of spiritual abundance just as there are laws of material abundance, one aspect of which is spiritual evolution and insight.

Spiritual life is always presented in the West as some kind of holy hobby, a free gift of the Heavenly Father to his indulged and obedient children. Not so. It is as much a livelihood as any worldly profession, and even more demanding. Spiritual attainment which empowers the aspirant for further spiritual endeavor is the coin, the needed asset, the "something" this verse is all about.

He who has in his hand, to him shall be given. One who actually possesses spiritual development in the sense that he can draw on it to help or guide him through life–use it in a very practical sense–will as a consequence be able to increase his store of spiritual power and proficiency. It is the nature of spiritual energy to increase by drawing more to itself, as a magnet draws iron. For this reason, those who carefully preserve their spiritual assets through steady spiritual practice and allow no diminishment or damage to them will find their spiritual treasury increasing automatically.

And he who has not, from him shall be taken even the little that he has. Sometimes a person suddenly comes into possession of a degree of spiritual awakening through the action of past karma or through the grace of God or a holy person. If such a one immediately acts on this good fortune and makes the spiritual power or impetus his own, it will be the beginning of his spiritual ascent. If not, the result will be very negative and he may have ruined his only spiritual chance for this lifetime or even future lifetimes.

One time Bishop Fulton Sheen was in Paris. He celebrated Mass in the famous Sacred Heart Church, and on his way out was stopped by a man who wanted to speak with a priest. Bishop Sheen invited him to breakfast, and the result was that they spent the entire day together with the man eagerly asking him about spiritual life. The man's intensity revealed that his situation was desperate. When they parted, Bishop Sheen agreed to meet with him the next morning at his hotel.

The next morning the man came to the hotel with a woman in tow, and proceeded to stand in the lobby and sneer at the bishop and mock all they had spoken about the day before. Then he turned and walked out without even a token farewell. The bishop understood: the man had met the woman and committed fornication with her the night before.

Heaven had slipped from his grasp and hell had gripped him. He had fallen into the abyss about which it has been said: "Between us and you there is a great gulf fixed: so that they which would pass from hence to you cannot; neither can they pass to us, that would come from thence" (Luke 16:26). He had become one of those "delivered into chains of darkness, to be reserved unto judgment" (II Peter 2:4). The word translated "judgment" is *krisis*, which means to become separated and cast out. Of course the man was not damned forever, but even temporary cutting off from spiritual opportunity results in confusion and suffering throughout this life at least. Such people do not need to die to go to hell, they are there already. When Bishop Sheen told of this incident he was deeply sad, but there was nothing he could do, "for whatsoever a man soweth, that shall he also reap" (Galatians 6:7).

"The little that he has" becomes nothing. Those who fall into this condition are those about whom God himself says: "Thou sayest, I am rich, and increased with goods, and have need of nothing; and knowest not that thou art wretched, and miserable, and poor, and blind, and naked" (Revelation 3:17).

MOVE ON

Jesus said, Become passers-by. (42)

The great Mughal emperor, Akhbar, in 1601 A.D. built a gate at Fatehpur Sikri on which he had written in Persian: "Jesus, son of Mary, said: The world is a Bridge, pass over it, but build no houses upon it." Simple wisdom, but not so easy to put into practice. Even though from birth we are witnessing the temporary character of everything in this world as well as the fact that everyone who comes into it through birth is inexorably moving toward the exit of death, we desperately hold on to things, situations and people, trying to make the raging stream of "change and decay all around I see" stop for us so we can feel safe and be without worry or fear.

The time must come when we heed and accept the assurance of the Bhagavad Gita: "Death is certain for the born. Rebirth is certain for the dead.... Before birth, beings are not manifest to our human senses. In the interim between birth and death, they are manifest. At death they return to the unmanifest again" (Bhagavad Gita 2:27-28). This is a Christian teaching, too, for Saint Paul tells us that "the fashion [*schema*: form] of this world passeth away" (I Corinthians 7:31). And Saint John says: "the world passeth away" (I John 2:17). Everything is breaking apart at different rates of speed. Water evaporates quickly and mountains last for millions of years, but everything disappears eventually. So if we lived for thousand or millions of years we would still be experiencing the perishable nature of all things. For the Gita also speaks of "mighty world-destroying Time" (11:32).

Actually, becoming "strangers and pilgrims" as Saint Paul and Saint Peter advise us (Hebrews 11:13; I Peter 2:11) is not noble or wise, it is just plain good sense, for that is all we ever are in this world. Our external lives and bodies break down and blow away just like everything and everyone else. If we try to go against this current of dissolution we will be overwhelmed and drowned in the flood and end in misery. If we acknowledge it and go along with it, learning the lessons it conveys, we have a chance of attaining peace.

The way is simple, actually: enter into and abide in the unchanging Spirit which is the source of all worlds and the source of us as well. Dwell in the unmoving center of all things: God. This is immortality.

"Therefore become a yogi" (Bhagavad Gita 6:46).

CHALLENGING
THE MASTER

His disciples said to him, Who are you, that you should say these things to us? [Jesus said to them,] You do not realize who I am from what I say to you, but you have become like the Judeans, for they (either) love the tree and hate its fruit (or) love the fruit and hate the tree. (43)

Jesus said, Whoever blasphemes against the Father will be forgiven, and whoever blasphemes against the Son will be forgiven, but whoever blasphemes against the Holy Spirit will not be forgiven either on earth or in heaven. (44)

His disciples said to him, Who are you, that you should say these things to us? In the eleventh chapter of the Bhagavad Gita the great warrior-yogi Arjuna apologizes to Krishna the great Master for having been disrespectful to him on occasions. It is not rare for disciples to lapse into ignorance and either ignore, disrespect or even challenge their teachers. This is really an expected thing, because on the path to enlightenment the ego begins to rebel, sensing its approaching death. Of course disrespect places the disciple in grave danger, for many disciples follow it up with abandoning the teacher and spiritual life. I have heard of some very terrible instances, and myself have witnessed some. So it is no small or light thing, and Jesus has some pungent words in response.

You do not realize who I am from what I say to you. Here is the heart of the matter. Over and over the great masters have told us that truth is never a matter of words, but direct realization. And that realization comes only to those who cultivate higher consciousness (which includes insight and understanding) through meditation and yogic discipline. Those who do not will not understand what they are being taught, and might as well not be trying. In the same way, without inner awakening no one can realize who or what the great masters really are. Every master or saint I have ever met was both regarded and disregarded by the people around them. This revealed who had an inner life of meditation and who did not. Just living with a holy person does absolutely nothing for those who are not cultivating their own holiness.

But you have become like the Judeans, for they [either] love the tree and hate its fruit [or] love the fruit and hate the tree. That is, they love wrongdoing but hate the painful consequences and want to avoid them while still doing wrong, or they like the idea of becoming masters themselves with all the blessings and advantages that brings, but they detest the disciplines, sacrifices and struggles that are required for attaining liberation and perfection. So they seek to get around what cannot be gotten around. Or they seek to be thought holy while still remaining unholy. (This last is the most popular strategy.) Jesus' disciples were in state of contradiction so they defied him and were searching a way around him, too.

Paramhansa Yogananda observed this around his exalted master, Swami Sri Yukteswar. He tells about it in the twelfth chapter of *Autobiography of a Yogi*: "Students came, and generally went. Those who craved a path of oily sympathy and comfortable recognitions did not find it at the hermitage. Master offered shelter and shepherding for the aeons, but many disciples miserly demanded ego-balm as well. They departed, preferring life's countless humiliations before any humility. Master's blazing rays, the open penetrating sunshine of his wisdom, were too powerful for their spiritual sickness. They sought some lesser teacher who, shading them with flattery, permitted the fitful sleep of ignorance."

Whoever blasphemes against the Father will be forgiven, and whoever blasphemes against the Son will be forgiven, but whoever blasphemes against the Holy Spirit will not be forgiven either on earth or in heaven. God as a Person, as Consciousness both transcendent (Father) and immanent (Son), is always merciful and forgiving, always ready to help those who ask in sincerity, whatever their past errors. But God as Power, as the Holy Spirit, the necessary deifying power inherent in the universe, cannot be defied, contradicted or ignored without incurring suffering and loss. This is the law of karma.

We all must return to the Absolute, but as long as we ignore and defy the irrevocable laws we will wander and suffer for lifetimes. It is not a matter of punishment, but of simple realities. If a child is warned not to touch a flame but does so, he will be burned and suffer—and will continue suffering every time he touches fire. The one who warned him is not punishing him, he is experiencing the natural consequence of his action. And in the case of spiritual life, if we go contrary to the ways of the deifying Holy Spirit the result will be disastrous. Our transgression can never be forgiven in the sense of one day no longer mattering.

Until we take up the required disciplines and make the required effort we will never be able to progress toward liberation. There is no waiving of the needed discipline and practice or a free passage upward, because it is a matter of evolution. We have to evolve and there is only one path of evolution. "Verily I say unto thee, thou shalt by no means come out thence, till thou hast paid the uttermost farthing" (Matthew 5:26), until all that is required of us to ascend to higher life has been done *in toto*—no shortcuts or cut rates. The choice is ours. We have God's blessing but we lack our own. A child cannot do what is required of an adult. No external well-wisher is going to change that. Growth and its attendant change is an absolute necessity. Again, the choice is ours.

THE SOURCE OF
GOOD AND EVIL

Jesus said, Grapes are not harvested from thorns, nor are figs gathered from thistles, for they do not produce fruit. A good man brings forth good from his storehouse; an evil man brings forth evil things from his evil storehouse, which is in his heart, and says evil things. For out of the abundance of the heart he brings forth evil things. (45)

Jesus said, Grapes are not harvested from thorns, nor are figs gathered from thistles, for they do not produce fruit. Even as children many of us heard older and wiser people say "Consider the source" when something–usually gossip–was being relayed. To determine the authenticity of anything we must find its source. Otherwise we may be fooled by the mere appearance of something. This is very much evident in today's "food industry." Consider all the fake food that people accept as equal to real food just because of the way it looks and tastes. And of course, some people prefer the synthetic to the authentic in all the departments of their life.

Only yesterday I read an excellent religious essay about how crucial it is to always check everything religious back to its roots. If its roots are not compatible with what it claims to be, or if it really has no roots, then it it not worthy of acceptance. This is why the concept of tradition as the basis of religion is so important. After all, tradition is absolutely cardinal in both science and civil law. Everything is built or based on something, and that foundation will determine the ultimate character of the superstructure. Therefore we need to check the genealogy of everything.

This does not mean that we must be slaves to the past in a mechanical, unreasoning manner, to think that the way something has been done is the only way to do it in the future, or that something that has not been done before is thereby untrustworthy. But where it comes from is crucial, because that will reveal its nature. The character of the source will be the essential character of the product. All that glitters is not gold, but not all gold glitters, either. We must do our best to understand the nature of all things relevant to us. Intelligence is not just a gift from God, it is a requisite without which we cannot live fully or rightly. So we must use it at all times and in all situations.

A good man brings forth good from his storehouse; an evil man brings forth evil things from his evil storehouse, which is in his heart, and says evil things. For out of the abundance of the heart he brings forth evil things. Patterson and Maeyer: "Good persons produce good from what they've stored up; bad persons produce evil from the wickedness they've stored up in their hearts, and say evil things. For from the overflow of the heart they produce evil."

The mind and heart are storehouses of a tremendous number and amount of things. We see from Jesus' words that we can only bring forth from our storehouse what has been put in there by us, however much we would like to blame others for many of the negative things hidden there. Much of what is stored up is either karma or conditioned by karma. So the bottom line is that we bring forth what is our own character, our acquired nature. If we don't like what is stored inside we must not deny or suppress it, but get in there and clear out the bad and bring in the good. In other words, we must meditate, for that is the only way to real interior renovation.

All the foregoing is speaking about the acquired nature, but our eternal nature is something completely different. We need to bring that forth, too, for that alone can endure. When we become on all levels what we have always been, then the goal is reached and freedom (moksha–liberation) is attained. As Buddha defined it: "The holy life has been lived, what had to be done has been done." Only the state of Nirvana remains for us. And yoga is the way.

GREAT IN THE KINGDOM

Jesus said, Among those born of women, from Adam until John the Baptist, there is no one so superior to John the Baptist that his eyes should not be lowered (before him). Yet I have said, whichever one of you comes to be a child will be acquainted with the kingdom and will become superior to John. (46)

The only way to become great in the kingdom of God is to enter it. How? When Jesus said: "Verily I say unto you, Except ye be converted, and become as little children, ye shall not enter into the kingdom of heaven" (Matthew 18:3), he was speaking of regaining our primal nature and condition of unity with God. The word translated "converted" is *strepho* which means to turn back in the sense of returning to where we were before. We must recover what the Zen Buddhists call our "original face." That is why as our example Jesus prayed: "O Father, glorify thou me with thine own self with the glory which I had with thee before the world was" (John 17:5). The path to perfection is the path of return. This, too, is the way of the yogi.

IMPOSSIBLE DUALITY

Jesus said, It is impossible for a man to mount two horses or to stretch two bows [at the same time]. And it is impossible for a servant to serve two masters; otherwise, he will honor the one and treat the other contemptuously.

No man drinks old wine and immediately desires to drink new wine. And new wine is not put into old wineskins, lest they burst; nor is old wine put into a new wineskin, lest it spoil it. An old patch is not sewn onto a new garment, because a tear would result. (47)

Impossibility

In all spiritual traditions throughout the world we find the teaching that there are two paths a person can walk: that which leads upward and that which leads downward, that which leads beyond this world and that which leads further into it. Obviously we cannot walk both paths at the same time. Those who hop from one to another continually will not get anywhere, nor will those who seek to somehow be in the middle. When the scale is in perfect balance it reads Zero. In Revelation we read: "I know thy works, that thou art neither cold nor hot: I would thou wert cold or hot. So then because thou art lukewarm, and neither cold nor hot, I will spue thee out of my mouth" (Revelation 3:15, 16). That is what God thinks of the much vaunted *via media*. He wants nothing to do with it. We should feel the same.

"Elijah came unto all the people, and said, How long halt ye between two opinions? if the Lord be God, follow him: but if Baal, then follow him. And the people answered him not a word" (I Kings 18:21). Unfortunately it has become the order of the day to dilly-dally and shilly-shally. Commitment seems to strike terror in the hearts of many people. Self-definition is absolutely shunned. Just today a friend sent us an email in which he said: "Everyone is content with the everyday littles." I would say that almost everyone *is* an everyday little by choice.

Those of us who want to accomplish something spiritually must make our choice and commit ourselves to it. We cannot be like Pilate who did not want to condemn Jesus but was too cowardly to release him. "When Pilate saw that he could prevail nothing, but that rather a tumult was made, he took water, and washed his hands before the multitude, saying, I am innocent of the blood of this just person: see ye to it.... and when he had scourged Jesus, he delivered him to be crucified" (Matthew 27:24, 26). So he did condemn Jesus. In the same way if we do not commit to spiritual life we choose the life of ego and ignorance. We honor that which opposes truth and dishonor that which leads to—and is—the truth. That which is not positively good is positively evil. This world is indeed made up of black and white—gray is just not seeing the reality of something.

"Enter ye in at the strait gate: for wide is the gate, and broad is the way, that leadeth to destruction, and many there be which go in thereat: because strait is the gate, and narrow is the way, which leadeth unto life, and few there be that find it" (Matthew 7:13, 14).

Old versus the new

The craze for the new and the contempt for the old grips the modern world. When Jesus speaks of old and new he is referring to the original divine order, including spiritual awareness as contrasted with the present confusion and disorder that both produces and is rooted in spiritual unconsciousness and indifference. Those who taste of the spiritual will lose all taste for the crassly material. Nor will they try to accommodate themselves to the times by altering and conforming the spiritual to the material, for that only leads to loss of the spiritual. The old and the new cannot coexist; by their nature they cancel one another. Those who pretend to be both are deceivers who mask the truth of their condition. Form without content, wells without water–such they are.

As with the matter of servant and master, there is no reconciliation, no timesharing arrangement. We are either building our life on the rock or on the sand (Matthew 7:24-27). It is impossible to do both simultaneously. Tragically there are those who really do not know which they are, blinded by both their ignorance and the words of those who "compass sea and land to make one proselyte, and when he is made, make him twofold more the child of hell than themselves" (Matthew 23:15). But when all is said and done, the choice is ours.

"Choose you this day whom ye will serve" (Joshua 24:15). To not choose is also a choice, as Pilate well knew.

PEACE THAT MOVES MOUNTAINS

Jesus said, If two make peace with each other in this one house, they will say to the mountain, "Move Away," and it will move away. (48)

This actually has two meanings, one outer and one inner.

Outer peace

It is very easy for people to be friends when they meet only occasionally in the right setting. Some families hardly know each other after years because they never really spend much time in one another's company. But when two people live together–really live together for many hours a day–they meet each other's quirks and flaws and the entire array of aberrations and peculiarities they have gathered over a long succession of lives. Considering the fact that this earth plane is the bottom rung of the evolutionary ladder it should not surprise us that prolonged exposure to one another does not conduce to endearment. Conflict is bound to arise and exasperation with one another's failings, not the least of which is egotism in its many forms. Often one of the two will be very passive and recessive and will suffer for decades without a word, often without even admitting to themselves what a misery their life has become. When this happens they have "a good relationship" or marriage or association. Of course it is no such thing at all, quite the opposite, but because no indications surface everyone (often even the sufferer) thinks all is well. The Bible tells us: "Blessed are the peacemakers" (Matthew 5:9), but such people do not have peace, only a ceasefire or stalemate. Peace at any price demands a terrible price, often the destruction of a soul.

It does not do if only one is a peacemaker, masking the ego and faults of the other. If, however, there is enough evolution and awakening on both sides, then harmony, understanding and profound love can result. It is these people that Jesus says can move mountains. For truly, in this troubled and unstable world peace is the greatest of miracles, and those who achieve it *together* deserve all praise and respect. The reason it does not occur more frequently is the unwillingness of people to make (create) it.

Inner peace

In the seventh chapter of Romans Saint Paul describes the intense conflict between his higher self and his lower self, between that part of him that gravitates to the spirit and that which reflects and is shaped–even enslaved–by the body and its material environment. The war between intelligence and instinct rages. Sri Ramakrishna said that he had seen within himself two persons (purusha), the man of evil (papa purusha) and the man of good (punya purusha). One of them, he said, must kill the other–there is no peaceful coexistence possible. Those who do nothing about this will find their good destroyed by their evil. Then they will have the sterile peace of death. Those who refuse to concede to their evil early on discover that they will have to fight to the death in the inner conflict. Only then can the peace of higher life be gained.

"He that is slow to anger is better than the mighty; and he that ruleth his spirit than he that taketh a city" (Proverbs 16:32). To win this conflict by truly destroying the roots of ignorance and evil is to be a god, a genuine miracle-worker. Such a one has already moved mountains, invisible though they be. It is also true that the mere word of such a one can banish all obstacles to future evolution. Theirs is "the peace of God which passeth all understanding" (Philippians 4:7).

BACK TO THE SOURCE

Jesus said, Blessed are the solitary and elect, for you will find the kingdom. For you are from it, and to it you will return. (49)

Jesus said, Blessed are the solitary and elect. Spiritual self-sufficiency is a cardinal trait of those who are going to succeed in spiritual life. Dependency on any but God (first) and ourselves (second) is harmful to us in every aspect of life, but especially in spiritual matters. Infantilism in religion has been popular throughout the ages because infants can be controlled completely and made into what the parents want. Enslavement in many forms is a natural aspect of ignorant human life.

Throughout history people have been slaves in countless ways, physical, mental and moral. But when Jesus speaks of being solitary or alone (as in some translations) he is not talking to hermits but to disciples that even then were engaged a great deal in contact with others as emissaries of Jesus in his mission. But they were solitary in that they were free from outer influence, having had their inner consciousness opened by Jesus and his teachings so only the inner light was their guide, and on that alone they depended to lead them to oneness with God–the sole true goal of human existence.

They were not slaves or servants of either Jesus or God, for Jesus said to them: "I call you not servants; for the servant knoweth not what his lord doeth: but I have called you *friends*; for all things that I have heard of my Father I have made known unto you" (John 15:15). Religion is riddled with enslavement, especially Eastern religion. See the spectacle of modern glitter-gurus and their slaves. But Jesus called his disciples *friends*–not disciples. And he told them they were *sons of God*, not servants. Paramhansa Yogananda, who publicly taught real Christianity in the twentieth century, taught people to pray: Heavenly Father, Divine Mother, *Friend, Beloved God*.

The elect are those that have been chosen by God and predestined for enlightenment: every single sentient being in all creation.

For you will find the kingdom, the kingdom regarding which Jesus said: "the kingdom of God is within you" (Luke 17:21). Jesus was a master yogi and his followers were yogis as well. Otherwise they could never have become blessed, self-sufficient, elect or friends and sons of God. Certainly, having opened their inner eyes and ears they would discover that blessed inner kingdom.

While writing the foregoing sentence I suddenly heard in my mind's ear a song I grew up singing at church:

> There's a theme that is sweet to my mem'ry,
> There's a joy that I cannot declare,
> There's a treasure that gladdens my being,
> 'Tis the kingdom of righteousness here.

We hadn't the faintest idea of what we were singing, but some years later when I read the Bhagavad Gita and *Autobiography of a Yogi* I found out the meaning and became a yogi to act on my newfound understanding.

For you are from it, and to it you will return. This is the major difference between Eastern and Western religion.

In the West any contact with God is a kind of intrusion on or break in normal life which has to be followed up by a complete overcoming of the natural order and forcing one's way to God on a perilous path from which anyone who falls, falls to their everlasting damnation.

In the East it is realized that contact with God, and any subsequent drawing nearer to God, is an expression of our eternal nature. That our very being is rooted in God and any separation from him in consciousness is abnormal, an interruption of the true order of things. Therefore to return to God is the most natural thing possible and is absolutely inevitable for God is our origin and our destiny. The question is not If, but When? It is a joyful return despite any snags occasioned by our lack of insight or understanding. Therefore the Catholic nun, Sister Maddaleva wrote:

Know you the journey that I take?
Know you the voyage that I make?
The joy of it—one's heart could break.

No jot of time have I to spare,
Nor will to loiter anywhere,
So eager am I to be there

For that the way is hard and long,
For that gray fears upon it throng,
I set my journey to the song.

And it grows wondrous happy so
Singing I hurry on for—oh!
It is to God, to God I go.

CHILDREN OF THE LIGHT

Ye are all the children of light, and the children of the day (I Thessalonians 5:5).

> Jesus said, If they say to you, "Where did you come from?" say to them, "We came from the light, the place where the light came into being on its own accord and established itself and became manifest through their image." If they say to you, "Is it you?," say, "We are its children, we are the elect of the living father." If they ask you, "What is the sign of your father in you?," say to them, "It is movement and repose." (50)

If they say to you, "Where did you come from?" say to them, "We came from the light, the place where the light came into being on its own accord and established itself and became manifest through their image." First let us note what Jesus does *not* tell us to say. He does not tell us to say that we are creations of God or servants or God–and certainly not sinners.

Our origin reveals our nature. Since we came from the Light, we are ourselves that Light. Quite some years ago a healing group met each week in our monastery. At the beginning of each session we would say some prayers, always ending with: "Christ is the Light; the Light is Christ. I am that Christ; I am that Light." This is the truth of our real, essential nature. It is not the truth of our temporal, ever-changing nature that is involved in evolution. But it is necessary for us to stop in our evolution dance occasionally and remember who and what we really are.

> Flower in the crannied wall,
> I pluck you out of the crannies,
> I hold you here, root and all, in my hand,
> Little flower–but if I could understand
> What you are, root and all, and all in all,
> I should know what God and man is.

So said Tennyson and so say all the wise. Those who do not say so should be ignored and even avoided. For they tell us lies about ourselves and would have us lie to ourselves in time. "Jesus answered and said unto them, Ye do err, not knowing the scriptures, nor the power of God" (Matthew 22:29). Saint Paul described them as "having a form of godliness, but denying the power thereof: *from such turn away*" (II Timothy 3:5).

We entered this relative field of evolution from "the place where the light came into being on its own accord and established itself and became manifest through their image." That is the point at which the Invisible Light became Visible Light so creation could be projected for our habitation and evolution. That Light manifested as the creation in which we too became manifest. Being images of God, we became revelations of God just as the sun is reflected in many vessels of water. The reflections are many, but the Reflected is One.

If they say to you, "Is it you?," say, "We are its children, we are the elect of the living father." We are not God, but we positively are the children of God, "for in him we live, and move, and have our being; for we are also his offspring" (Acts 17:28). The word translated "offspring" is *genos*, which means "kind" and from which we get the word *genus*–species. So we are what God is–as Tennyson says above–the difference being in degree. God is infinite and we are finite, he is the ocean and we are the waves. The ocean is the wave, but the wave is not the ocean.

We have been chosen by God, the Living Father, to evolve throughout our incarnations within relative creation, within physical, astral and causal worlds, until we attain to his perfect likeness, participating in his infinity which he shares with us, yet which is always his exclusively. We become godlike but never become God. We will be gods within God.

If they ask you, "What is the sign of your father in you?," say to them, "It is movement and repose." Our life is the shared life of God. It is a dynamic, evolutionary life which consists of "movement and repose," of "motion and rest" (Patterson and Maeyer's translation). This means that within us there is both intense evolutionary movement in the form of development and at the same time there is an increasing establishment and expansion in the motionless consciousness that is the essence of our being, that is the Father within us. These two simultaneous poles of our existence are the "sign" of our Father within us.

Here, too, the words of Rumi cited earlier apply. This is the heart-song and the experience of the yogi.

HERE AND NOW

His disciples said to him, When will the repose of the dead come about, and when will the new world come? He said to them, What you look forward to has already come, but you do not recognize it. (51)

This is not a new phenomenon. People often miss something very important and do not know it. So they keep waiting for it to happen when it is long past. This is especially true when they have expected something internal to be an external event or when something symbolic or psychological was thought to be a very overt and visible incident. For example, many spiritual teachers have said for over a century now that "Armageddon" is being fought at this very moment on the inner planes of the spirit and will never be a visible war. In religion especially there is a very real risk of thinking something is a symbol when it will be literal, and literal when it will be symbolic. And most of all we see the tragic effects of misunderstanding the nature of Christ and the Kingdom.

Therefore we must be careful to look back at what is behind and forward to what is in the future. And always to scrutinize the present lest we miss something great by looking for it in the wrong place or time.

SEEING YET BLIND

His disciples said to him, Twenty-four prophets spoke in Israel, and all of them spoke of you. He said to them, You have omitted the one living in your presence and have spoken (only) of the dead. (52)

There are various speculations about the identity of the "twenty-four prophets," none of which carry much weight. I think we can be satisfied with the "coincidence" that in Hindu scriptures twenty-four incarnations of Vishnu are enumerated, and twenty-four Tirthankaras (liberated masters) in the Jain scriptures. The real point is that the disciples had in mind prophets who were embodied in the past, forgetting that Jesus himself in his previous lives as Abraham, Moses, David and Isaiah spoke of his messianic advent as Jesus and was now the Prophet living with them and teaching them.

It is a common failing of religion to look to the past or the future with minimal attention given to the here-and-now of spiritual matters. But Jesus is pointing out that neither past nor future are present realities with practical meaning for those who choose to seek God now. Seekers of divine consciousness should not ignore past and future, but they should be intent on what is going on in their spiritual life right now—not yesterday or tomorrow. "Behold, now is the accepted time; behold, now is the day of salvation" (II Corinthians 6:2). "Wherefore as the Holy Ghost saith, To day if ye will hear his voice,… exhort one another daily, while it is called To day…. For we are made partakers of Christ, if we hold the beginning of our confidence stedfast unto the end; while it is said, To day if ye will hear his voice (Hebrews 3:7, 13-15)… Seek ye the Lord while he may be found, call ye upon him while he is near" (Isaiah 55:6).

OUTER RITUAL OR
INNER GROWTH?

His disciples said to him, Is circumcision beneficial or not?
He said to them, If it were beneficial, their father would beget
them already circumcised from their mother. Rather, the true
circumcision in spirit has become completely profitable. (53)

It was a wonder to me from childhood that a spiritual meaning, much
less value, could be attributed to bodily mutilation perpetrated on
an infant by its own parents. The members of the church I was brought
up in laughed at the idea that certain ritual acts of other churches were
believed to have literal effects, yet they accepted that circumcision was
somehow a spiritual action that produced a spiritual effect. The whole
thing was incredible. But let us turn from that to the teaching of Jesus
regarding these matters.

Anyone who has contact with modern conservative Christianity is
aware that a cornerstone of belief is the assertion that the Bible contains
within itself all that is needful for salvation. The history of Protestantism
proves conclusively that this does not work. And so does the experience
of myself and every Protestant I grew up with, however devout.

The truth–which was long ago officially condemned by exoteric Christianity under the label of Pelagianism–is that human beings, who are in the image and likeness of God (Genesis 1:26), have within themselves everything needed for their spiritual perfection (salvation). That is, liberation (salvation) is inherent in each one of us. This is the universal teaching of the East, Hindu, Buddhist and Taoist. And it is the teaching of authentic Christianity which came to us from the East through Jesus Christ. (See *The Christ of India*.)

Just as a seed when planted and watered correctly will grow into a mature plant, so the individual spirit will grow and manifest its innate divinity when the right inner and outer conditions are sufficiently supplied. Those who are inwardly awakened and develop the capacity for conscious self-evolution and diligently apply that ability will understand the declaration of Saint John the Apostle: "Beloved, now are we the sons of God, and it doth not yet appear what we shall be: but we know that, when he shall appear, we shall be like him; for we shall see him as he is. And every man that hath this hope in him purifieth himself, even as he is pure" (I John 2:2-3). In other words, he becomes a yogi and is revealed as a divine son of God, a Christ, as was Jesus.

Only the inner life is the true life.

INFINITE TRANSCENDENCE

Jesus said, Blessed are the poor, for yours is the kingdom of heaven. (54)

The Kingdom of Heaven is not a place or a thing, but a state of being: the state of Divine Being. And since divinity is beyond all relativity, beyond all things, only the "poor"–the absolutely possessionless and attributeless–attain that kingdom. It is the blessedness of No-Thing which is in reality the blessedness of Everything. Those who have nothing of this illusory existence are able to "possess the land" of Infinity forever.

"The saints of the most High shall take the kingdom, and possess the kingdom for ever, even for ever and ever" (Daniel 7:18).

"And he said unto him, Son, thou art ever with me, and all that I have is thine" (Luke 15:31).

"HATE"

Jesus said, Whoever does not hate his father and his mother cannot become a disciple to me. And whoever does not hate his brothers and sisters and take up his cross in my way will not be worthy of me. (55)

There can be a great deal of confusion in understanding passages in the Bible that contain the world "hate." Even though the Gospel of Thomas is only found in Coptic and fragmentary Greek texts, I believe a look at the Greek word translated "hate" in the New Testament will assist us.

The word in Greek is *miseo*, which has various shades of meaning. Certainly what we mean by hate is part of the meaning, but whenever it involves an opinion or judgment about a person or situation, especially a comparison, then it changes entirely to an expression of relative valuation or regard. It can mean to think less of something, but it also can mean to completely disregard something, for something to be as nothing in a person's opinion.

In Luke we find this: "If any man come to me, and hate not his father, and mother, and wife, and children, and brethren, and sisters, yea, and his own life also, he cannot be my disciple" (Luke 14:26). What Jesus is saying here is that in spiritual life everything must be secondary to that life. If there is conflict or even competition with it then we must ensure that everything beside spiritual life is nothing to us, even nonexistent. It may take an intense act of will if there is deep attachment to whatever rivals our spiritual pursuit, but it must be done.

Jesus is the perfect example: he totally disregarded his life and laid it down for the salvation of mankind. Instead of disregarding others, he disregarded himself, sacrificing himself willingly so that others might gain conscious, eternal life in freedom of spirit.

Since a great deal in the Gospels is symbolic, we can also think of father, mother, brothers and sisters as the elements that make up or influence our personal, ego-centered life, that they symbolize anything to which an attachment may arise that will distract or even draw us away from our spiritual aspirations. Such an ideal is essential for our success in divine attainment.

TRUE UNDERSTANDING

Jesus said, Whoever has come to understand the world has found (only) a corpse, and whoever has found a corpse is superior to the world. (56)

This is extremely clear. The only question is whether the reader will believe it or not, and to what degree.

The principle is also clear: Spirit is life, is all; and that which is not spirit is dead, is nothing. The world, being an expression of Spirit must in actuality be alive, but if the individual person is unaware of Spirit as the source and essence of the world, then for him the world is dead–worse, it is deadly. In the motion picture *Little Big Man*, the old chief says to his adopted grandson played by Dustin Hoffman: "The white man believes that the world is dead, and after a while he believes that he is dead." A materialistic view of the world breeds a materialistic, soulless view of oneself and of others. This is the horror of Marxist Dialectical Materialism as we saw lived out in the Soviet Union for so long.

But there is a practical aspect to this. We have to "ensoul" the world by awakening our own spirit consciousness. When we do that we will see that it is overflowing with life–divine life–that for the awakened person experience of the world is experience, even a revelation, of the spirit. But for the unawake it remains dead and purposeless.

When we understand that the world of itself is nothing, that it is an expression of divinity, and therefore at the same time everything, then we have risen above corpse consciousness into God consciousness. Infinity is ours.

WHEAT AND WEEDS

Jesus said, The kingdom of the father is like a man who had good seed. His enemy came by night and sowed weeds among the good seed. The man did not allow them to pull up the weeds; he said to them, 'I am afraid that you will go intending to pull up the weeds and pull up the wheat along with them.' For on the day of the harvest the weeds will be plainly visible, and they will be pulled up and burned. (57)

For many ages throughout the world, whatever the spiritual tradition might be, a question has persisted: "Why is there both good and evil in the world? Why do good and evil people live together on the earth, seemingly in equal status and fortune, and the evil often being the more fortunate? How can this be if God is truly good?" The answer is contained in that question itself. The situation is itself a manifestation of the goodness of God.

The world is not a kind of artificial structure meant to be beautiful and impressive–or even perfect to the observer. Rather it is a vast field of evolutionary life on infinite levels and grades in which each evolving consciousness (spirit) is finding its way upward to ultimate perfection. This is an agelong process whose length and course is determined completely by the individual spirit. Duality being an essential element of relative existence, naturally there will be a moving back and forth from that which facilitates evolution and that which hinders or reverses it. That, and that alone, is what determines good and evil. Good advances evolution and evil slows, stops or reverses it. It is not a matter of God's arbitrary will, but the will of the evolving entity itself as it passes from form to form on the evolutionary scale.

Problems arise on both the paths, upward and downward, but since the impulse to evolution is within the very essence of the spirit, self-correction will eventually occur. This is a most important fact. If long enough time passes, even though it be for countless creation cycles, the goal of perfection as an awakened god within God will be reached permanently.

Do Jesus' words give a picture of the world created by God but maliciously flawed by the Devil or Satan? No. There is a negative force that many identify with those names, but that, too, is a necessary and inherent part of creation. For a very full explanation of this, see *The Second Coming of Christ* by Paramhansa Yogananda.

The whole idea of this parable is that it is the nature of the world for there to be positive and negative, light and dark, good and evil. Neither must be interfered with (though good can be encouraged and evil discouraged once the evolving being has reach a degree of self-awareness). Rather, they must be left alone until that which is good and true in each individual has been realized and that which is evil and false has been eliminated—cast out and burnt in the fire of divine realization (consciousness). No person will ever be rejected or burnt, only that which is extraneous and not-self. The spirit shall be released into perfect freedom.

"Now is come salvation, and strength, and the kingdom of our God, and the power of his Christ" (Revelation 12:10).

FINDING LIFE

Jesus said, Blessed is the man who has suffered and found life. (58)

Considering how consistently esoteric the viewpoint of the Gospel of Thomas is, I feel we can be assured that this is not an extension of the "suffering purifies and ennobles" cliché and the virtual obsession of conservative exoteric Christianity that exalts misery and death. Certainly Jesus spoke of taking up the cross in the form of denying our lower self and passing from the illusory life that is really death into the true life that the deluded consider death (Matthew 16:24). There is no doubt that this involves pain to the ego and to that part of us that must be purified from ego and its errant ways. So suffering is indeed part of seeking and finding life. This Jesus implies by saying that those who mourn and hunger and thirst are blessed (Matthew 5:4, 6).

Personally I consider that struggle is meant here instead of ordinary suffering. Patterson and Maeyer perhaps agree with me, because they render it: "Jesus said, Congratulations to the person who has toiled and has found life." For it does indeed involve labor to first divest ourselves of what hinders us and then put on that which will enable us to "run with patience the race that is set before us, looking unto Jesus the author

166

and finisher of our faith; who for the joy that was set before him endured the cross, despising the shame, and is set down at the right hand of the throne of God" (Hebrews 12:1, 2). "Lay hold on eternal life, whereunto thou art also called" (I Timothy 6:12).

LIVE AND DIE NOT

Jesus said, Take heed of the living one while you are alive, lest you die and seek to see him and be unable to do so. (59)

Take heed of the living one. "The living one" can mean the Living God, our own living spirit and the Living Path–the life that leads to Life. Certainly all three should be kept in mind as we live our little life within the Infinite Life that is manifesting as the cosmos.

Only this morning there suddenly came to mind a blessed day over fifty years ago when a friend and I rode up the freeway north of Los Angeles singing Yogananda's chant:

I am the sky, Mother, I am the sky.
I am the vast blue ocean of sky.
I am a little drop of that sky.
Frozen sky....

The joyous vibrations Yogananda had infused into those words were flowing in our hearts. We did not even quit singing when we stopped for gas! But it was not just the feeling: the profound meaning was also rising in our awareness as we sang.

The words seem simple, and to some perhaps childish, but they are not. In the chant the devotee is speaking to the Divine Mother within whose cosmic heart he is living and evolving. Here in this seemingly material universe (that is really God's Light), we think we are in a purely material body, and we mostly identify with it. But in the chant the devotee is saying: "No, Mother, your motion picture creation will not fool me. I am not a mere body subject to birth and death; and though I dream karma, I am truly ever-free. Like your child Shankara sang in his *Stanzas on Nirvana*: I am formed of blissful consciousness: I am Spirit.

"I am myself the Chidakasha, the vast Conscious Ether of Space, the limitless Sky of Infinity. Thou art the Ocean Sky and I am a little drop in that Sky. Though momentarily frozen into a form, I am not limited to it. And as a yogi I am returning to my original state as part of–one with–Thee who art also beyond all form and name. For That Thou art and That am I."

For nearly an hour we were so in touch with that experience that we spent the rest of our life seeking to become established in it.

While you are alive, lest you die. No human being is a stranger to delusion, but one of the saddest I have observed is the mistaken belief that a person has their entire life to begin spiritual endeavor–that they can delay and delay all they want, even years if not decades, and still God and the angels will be waiting for them to get on board and make the journey. But anyone who has observed life knows that things go in cycles or tides. Even a single day can make a tremendous difference in a person's circumstances, inner and outer. Spiritual awakening and insight can be very fragile. I have seen it melt away without people even realizing it.

In past centuries, including Biblical times, a great deal that eventually became duties of officials such as soldiers and police was put into the hands of the ordinary people. For example, captured soldiers were often put into the custody of citizens who would be executed if the prisoner managed to escape. In the First Book of Kings a prophet in disguise goes to the king and tells him that someone brought a prisoner to him and warned him that he would pay with his life if the man got away. But, he tells the king, "as thy servant was busy here and there, he was gone" (I Kings 20:40). Just like that! When the king tells him that his life is forfeit, he then reveals who he is and tells the king that it is he who is accountable with his life because he shirked his duty to God. How easy it is to be busy here and there and lose track of our own Self.

And seek to see him and be unable to do so. No one is "lost" or "damned" forever, but certainly times can come when a person cannot take up spiritual life and progress, either because they have completely lost interest or because conditions no longer allow it. That is why the prophet said: "Seek ye the Lord while he may be found, call ye upon him while he is near" (Isaiah 55:6).

Some people decide to start spiritual life but begin looking in the wrong place, get distracted and wander into byways that are spiritual dead ends or they try to live a spiritual life while still avidly seeking material life. As the angel said to those who came to Jesus' tomb on the first Easter: "Why seek ye the living among the dead?" (Luke 24:5).

It is no joke. The words of Jesus often apply: "Then said Jesus unto them, Yet a little while am I with you, and then I go unto him that sent me. Ye shall seek me, and shall not find me: and where I am, thither ye cannot come" (John 7:33, 34). Then the lament may arise: "The harvest is past, the summer is ended, and we are not saved [liberated]" (Jeremiah 8:20).

"Lest Thou Also…"

[They saw] a Samaritan carrying a lamb on his way to Judea.
He said to his disciples, That man is round about the lamb.

They said to him, So that he may kill it and eat it.

He said to them, While it is alive, he will not eat it, but only
when he has killed it and it has become a corpse.

They said to him, He cannot do so otherwise.

He said to them, You too, look for a place for yourself within
repose, lest you become a corpse and be eaten. (60)

Intent on death

This verse has two vital messages. The first is indicated by Jesus'
words: "That man is round about the lamb." The man was carrying
the lamb in such a way that he was wrapped around it, encompassing
it, making it the center of his attention. But his intention was to kill
and eat it. In the same way, filled with ignorance and ruled by ego,
whatever the ordinary human being sets his attention and desire upon
becomes an extension of his inner state of spiritual death, and rather
than giving him life actually compounds his "death" condition. Realizing this, Shelley wrote:

Lift not the painted veil which those who live
Call Life: though unreal shapes be pictured there,
And it but mimic all we would believe
With colours idly spread,—behind, lurk Fear
And Hope, twin Destinies; who ever weave
Their shadows, o'er the chasm, sightless and drear.
I knew one who had lifted it—he sought,
For his lost heart was tender, things to love,
But found them not, alas! nor was there aught
The world contains, the which he could approve.
Through the unheeding many he did move,
A splendour among shadows, a bright blot
Upon this gloomy scene, a Spirit that strove
For truth, and like the Preacher found it not.

The unawakened who "seize life" really seize death.

Seek safety and life

"You too, look for a place for yourself within repose, lest you become a corpse and be eaten." It is not what we mistake for life that we should seek, but rather we should seek for the rest, the repose, that can only be found when we are centered in spirit rather than the shadow we call "the world." When we turn within and find the life and peace that is the core of our being, then we will be alive and never again be "dead" or "eaten."

WHO WILL DIE;
WHO WILL LIVE

Jesus said, Two will rest on a bed: the one will die, and the other will live.

Salome said, Who are you, man, that you... have come up on my couch and eaten from my table?

Jesus said to her, I am he who exists from the undivided. I was given some of the things of my father.

[...] I am your disciple.

[...] Therefore I say, if he is destroyed, he will be filled with light, but if he is divided, he will be filled with darkness. (61)

Relative existence consists of dualities, including life and death. Although we think of death as opposed to life, as canceling it out, it is actually an essential part of life. For in truth everything is Life because everything is a manifestation of the Divine in whom there is no real death. What we think is death is only a change. Therefore in the ancient texts of the Mass for the Departed we find the words: "Unto thy faithful, O Lord, life is changed, not taken away...."

Nevertheless, the appearance of death is always with us in the form of drastic change. For this reason Jesus enunciates the cosmic law that some will die and some will live in a perpetual sequence of change. There are none that live that will not die and none that die that will not live. Those of earth-dimmed vision are always troubled by this assertion, as was Salome who demanded to know who Jesus was that he could seemingly lay down this inflexible law that brings fear and sorrow to nearly all.

Spiritual teachers of all ages have been challenged with the words: "Who are you?" Many are the answers that have been given, including silence. Here we are told at least one reply Jesus gave to the demand, an answer that we all can give even now, though more fully in the future. His reply is twofold: "I am he who exists from the undivided." And: "I was given some of the things of my father."

Although we are dreaming the dream of separation, in reality we are rooted in the very being of the Undivided Reality, Satchidananda Brahman. We did not "come" from That, we are living in That as an eternal and inseparable part of That. That is why in the Chandogya Upanishad Uddalaka keeps saying to his son Svetaketu: THAT THOU ART. As simple as it is true.

We are not the Father, the Absolute, but being part of That we are also like That in some ways. That is our "inheritance" so to speak, which is why Jesus says: "I was given *some of the things* of my father."

These two facets of our identity should ever be kept in mind.

Finally Jesus gives us a fundamental principle regarding enlightenment. We do not attain enlightenment, we uncover it in the depths of our being–or we do not, and practically speaking remain unenlightened. But it is essential to realize that no one becomes enlightened, but rather discovers the Light is already present within.

The translation seems strange, but it means that those whose illusory shell is being dissolved and whose age-long wrong identity is being destroyed are on the way to experience enlightenment. But Patterson and Maeyer render it more clearly: "For this reason I say, if one is (whole), one will be filled with light, but if one is divided, one will be filled with darkness." If we are one, as is the Father, then like the Father we will find that we are totally Light. But if we are in the illusion of division, of duality, then we will see only darkness–even if we mistake it for the Light.

"The light of the body is the eye: if therefore thine eye be single, thy whole body shall be full of light. But if thine eye be evil, thy whole body shall be full of darkness. If therefore the light that is in thee be darkness, how great is that darkness!" (Matthew 6:22, 23). By "eye" is meant our consciousness. If our eye is single, is one, then we are full of light. But if it is divided, is dual, then it is full of darkness. And if we mistake that darkness for light, how great indeed it will be. Most people live in that state, which is why Krishna said: "Truly this maya of mine made of the gunas is difficult to go beyond. Verily only those who attain me shall pass beyond this maya" (Bhagavad Gita 7:14). Those who seek God alone shall seek and find–none other.

THE PATH OF
UNKNOWING

Jesus said, It is to those who are worthy of my mysteries that I tell my mysteries. Do not let your left (hand) know what your right (hand) is doing. (62)

It is to those who are worthy of my mysteries that I tell my mysteries. These are not the words of a teacher, however worthy, but the words of a divine messenger and therefore the words that God would speak. The idea is that nothing comes to the evolving individual before the time–and that includes insight and intuition. Until evolution opens the eyes, no one sees. God does not waste time with those incapable of both coping with and utilizing knowledge for their betterment. When someone is shown something either directly by God or through an intermediary, it is because they have evolved to a point that they would have figured it out on their own anyway. It is commonly said that a bank will not loan you money unless you can prove you do not need it. In the same way, divine revelation comes to those whose inner divinity would have imparted it to them directly. It is a version of "It gets light just before the sun comes up." It is a precursor of what would arise naturally in the consciousness. Nothing happens before the time, and nothing that is to happen can be prevented, because it is a matter of development, or natural unfoldment.

I can give an example. When I came back a monk from my first trip to India, every spiritual bully that had momentarily aspired to monastic life and then gotten married was very spiteful and contemptuous of me. As if they all had a script they would make snide remarks about being a monk inwardly, not just outwardly; wearing the gerua inside rather than outside. The implication was that I was just showing off. This got very wearisome, and when I had the blessing of meeting the great royal kahuna David (Daddy) Bray of Hawaii I was so gun-shy that when he took my hands, smiled radiantly, and said: "So you wear the robes," I answered: "I hope I wear them inwardly." He positively beamed at me and said: "Oh, if you did not have them inside you would not be wearing them outside!" Sweet relief! And I never again wavered in the face of those who resented my doing what they knew they should have done.

Yogananda's greatest disciple, Sister Gyanamata, once wrote to a nun: "Your own will always come to you. Indeed, you can have nothing but your own." There is no coincidence, happenstance or luck: it is all Law. When it is yours you get it; when it is not, you do not. In the divine realm the unworthy get nothing and the worthy always get what they need.

Do not let your left (hand) know what your right (hand) is doing. In the Gospel of Matthew we find: "When thou doest alms, let not thy left hand know what thy right hand doeth: that thine alms may be in secret" (Matthew 6:3, 4). Here, too, in this context it is secrecy that is being enjoined. This is a most crucial directive, because it is the habit of the ego-gripped person to trumpet abroad any and all insights or revelations–supposedly from a higher source, when they are only from their foolish mind. It has been very common for self-created visionaries and mystics to keep elaborately detailed diaries of every little breeze that ruffled their ambition-fevered mind in hope that they would be accidentally discovered during their lifetime or at least after their death. Then sainthood might be declared!

From the Middle Ages on, Western Christianity has been plagued by these people, whose interminable revelations have won for them a throne in heaven–at least in the minds of the gullible and those who have themselves also aspired to such honor. Some of these revelations have been obviously fabricated and others have proceeded from a truly deranged mentality. One very famous medieval mystic described a long series of visions that are exactly like mescaline hallucinations. Obviously something was wrong with her brain chemistry. Quite a number of obviously psychotic women (usually nuns) have been formally canonized on the basis of such delusions. I have read a few biographies of nuns whose "cause is pending" who quite obviously were keeping the other members of their convent hopping to the tune of their continuous revelations. Almost daily updates on mystical revelations kept the pot boiling and stirring. Of course, once the "infallible magisterium" of the Church declared these fantasies or fabrications real, then any sensible scrutiny became impossible and even a blasphemy.

True mystics keep silence because their experiences are between them and God alone. Dom Cuthbert Butler in *Benedictine Monachism* has presented a little known fact. Until the "flowering" of the Middle Ages and the rise of profoundly personal (*i.e.* ego-centered) mysticism with its attendant revelations, there was quite literally only one form of mystical experience that was considered authentic: the vision of the Divine Uncreated Light in which the mystic clearly realized that he was one with that Light in total spiritual union. In other words, a true mystic had two simultaneous experiences: seeing Divine Light and knowing he was one with the Light, that Unity alone was true and duality a delusion. That was the sum of the matter.

Many kinds of visions are possible that are real and have a purpose. But the purpose is almost always private. They are messages from on high, but the highest mystical experience, the revelation of God, is just what Dom Cuthbert specifies: Oneness with the Divine Light. Such experiences did happen during the Middle Ages and after, but they did not catch what is known as "the popular imagination." No surprise. Nevertheless, Saint Bernard saw the entire universe and God as a single beam of Light. In the Christian East, Saint Symeon the New Theologian also viewed the Uncreated Light and knew that it was inseparable from him, that he existed in it and was one with it. Richard Rolle of England, despite the raging fantasies current in his day, wrote that it was the vision of the Uncreated Light such as the apostles beheld at the transfiguration of Jesus that was the only true spiritual experience.

I am laboring this point, but that is because in this information age people now have access to the psychic aberrations of supposed mystics of all religions East and West. If I cited for you some of the things that Western yogis have told me with great confidence as spiritual experiences you would not believe me, they are so silly and crazy.

The only thing further for me to say is that in the Bhagavad Gita alone can we find a description of genuine enlightenment as a purely subjective experience that no outsider can know or declare either real or false. Only the illumined know if they are such. That is why Yogananda simply said: "He who knows—he knows. None else knows."

AWAKENED BY DEATH

Jesus said, There was a rich man who had much money. He said, 'I shall put my money to use so that I may sow, reap, plant, and fill my storehouse with produce, with the result that I shall lack nothing.' Such were his intentions, but that same night he died. Let him who has ears hear. (63)

We are not just immortal, we are eternal, and even though our experience in this world seems to contradict that completely, nevertheless we have a subconscious awareness that we are essentially unchanging beings. This, however can lead to trouble, because we then tend to react to a temporary situation as though it were really permanent. Whether it be pleasant or unpleasant, we reflexively react as though it will last forever. Consequently we panic or overreact in a manner completely inconsistent with the reality of the situation when things are unpleasant, or unrealistically insist to ourselves that anything which we like will always be ours.

Death is one of the most powerful and upsetting intruders in our complacency. We think we will be young, healthy, wealthy, loved and content forever. Many things can overturn this mistaken conclusion, but death is the most shocking for there is no way to deny its absolutely irrevocable nature and effect on us. The death of others usually shakes us awake to a more reasonable view of things, but our own death can really change our viewpoint. That is what Jesus is explaining here.

Everything conduced to make the rich man content and assured. No doubt or fear clouded his mental horizons. Just the opposite: he felt that the cosmos itself could not bring about any detrimental change or diminish his total confidence in a future that would be exactly as he wished it to be, as well as unending. But suddenly he found himself in another realm of existence altogether where there were no such things as fields, crops or storehouses. To his mind, he had lost everything, since all he had filled his mind with for a lifetime had been objective, material things. Now he had no possessions whatsoever—just himself. And that was a very flimsy and unsatisfactory inventory indeed!

Death forces us to acknowledge a multitude of realities that we do not want to face, mostly because we do not want to adjust our thinking and behavior according to the way things really are—or are not. Many years ago I had a book of hymns that contained one entitled "With Eternity's Values in View." Many people may think that keeping death and our personal mortality in mind is morbid, but it is not if we order our life and thought in conformity with those realities. We cannot have life without death, or death without life. Those who acknowledge that principle and make provision for all possibilities will never have to be evicted by death before facing reality. There will be no surprises; only fulfillments. This Jesus is demonstrating to us.

Turning Ourselves Away

Jesus said, A man had received visitors. And when he had prepared the dinner, he sent his servant to invite the guests.

He went to the first one and said to him, 'My master invites you.' He said, 'I have claims against some merchants. They are coming to me this evening. I must go and give them my orders. I ask to be excused from the dinner.'

He went to another and said to him, 'My master has invited you.' He said to him, 'I have just bought a house and am required for the day. I shall not have any spare time.'

He went to another and said to him, 'My master invites you.' He said to him, 'My friend is going to get married, and I am to prepare the banquet. I shall not be able to come. I ask to be excused from the dinner.'

He went to another and said to him, 'My master invites you.' He said to him, 'I have just bought a farm, and I am on my way to collect the rent. I shall not be able to come. I ask to be excused.'

The servant returned and said to his master, 'Those whom you invited to the dinner have asked to be excused.' The master said to his servant, 'Go outside to the streets and bring back those

whom you happen to meet, so that they may dine.' Businessmen and merchants will not enter the places of my father. (64)

There is a lot of talk about free will, but almost none about the responsibility it entails. Because of our experiences from life to life we tend to project onto God what is really only found among limited humanity. As children we have no say in matters: what we get, we get, and what we do not get, we do not get. So it is assumed that it is the same with God: God either gives, refuses or takes away and we have no input whatsoever. But that is wrong. We get what we bring to ourselves by deed and thought. If the right kind of thought and action is not supplied, then it does not occur. We are always in complete charge. God has extended this universe and it operates according to the law of cause and effect which is completely in our hands though we usually do not realize it.

God can offer, but we can refuse. That is what this parable is all about. Lest we deny ourselves something we want, Jesus is showing us the way things really work so we will not blame God rather than ourselves when things do not go as we wish.

In the Gospel of Saint Luke 14:16-24, the reasons people give to excuse themselves from spiritual life and responsibility are given, but here Jesus is revealing the attitudes that bar us from the material and spiritual bounty God would bestow on us. All four excuses deal with money, property, and social obligations. When things and people are uppermost in our minds and hearts we deny ourselves much that could easily be ours. We make no room in our lives for God.

The summation is in the words: "Businessmen and merchants will not enter the places of my father." Those who make a living rather than make a life, who deal with both earthly life and spiritual life as though they were based on account books, render themselves incapable of relating to either God or man in a meaningful or realistic manner. But especially they alienate themselves from all higher life. Not realizing that material life is only temporary and meant to be eventually left behind, whereas spiritual life is meant to be our permanent future, people render themselves unfit for this life and the next. As a consequence they lose both lives and flounder around from life to life in this unstable and unsatisfying world. Only when things change in their hearts will anything change in their destiny.

GULLIBILITY

He said, There was a good man who owned a vineyard. He leased it to tenant farmers so that they might work it and he might collect the produce from them. He sent his servant so that the tenants might give him the produce of the vineyard. They seized his servant and beat him, all but killing him. The servant went back and told his master. The master said, 'Perhaps they did not recognize him.' He sent another servant. The tenants beat this one as well. Then the owner sent his son and said, 'Perhaps they will show respect to my son.' Because the tenants knew that it was he who was the heir to the vineyard, they seized him and killed him. Let him who has ears hear. (65)

A similar parable is found in the Gospels of Matthew and Mark, but they are clearly about the rejection of Jesus as Messiah by the people of Israel. This is quite different, being about a flaw in personal judgment of a life situation.

Sometimes goodness can hinder a person rather than further them. I know that sounds strange, but I have seen how extremely truthful and guileless people can easily be fooled by liars because it never crosses their mind that someone might be lying to them. My maternal grandmother was just such a person. Though highly intelligent, since she had grown up in a family where truthfulness was always observed and she herself had always been honest and open, anyone could hoodwink her, even the most blatant fakes.

The good man of this parable was kind and easygoing. Therefore when his tenants beat the man sent to collect the rent in the form of produce, he made excuse for them, saying: "Perhaps they did not recognize him," which is really stretching it to beyond the breaking point. In fact, it is simply being foolish and not in the least virtuous. Those who do not confront evil and name it for what it is are themselves collaborators with that evil.

But the story does not end there. The same thing happened again. And instead of realizing that his tenants were criminals that needed harsh punishment, he sent his son, naively thinking that they would not do the same to him. And they did not: they killed him. So the father was as guilty of his son's death as were they. This is plain fact.

Many times people tolerate outrageous behavior in the form of insults and injury. For years they keep saying to themselves: "They don't realize what they are doing," thinking they are following the example of Jesus when he prayed: "Father, forgive them; for they know not what they do" (Luke 23:34). So this kind of nonsense can go on for years–until finally the message gets through: those people knew exactly what they were doing because they were evil and had evil intent toward us. It is the fault of those who blindly excuse them.

Being ready to see and name evil, we no longer suffer from it. So if peace is desired, then the willingness to give the boot to evil can prevent its incursion into our lives. This s a hard lesson to learn, and I hope what I have written will help you avoid a lot of pain and frustration.

THE REJECTED IS
TRULY ACCEPTED

Jesus said, Show me the stone which the builders have rejected. That one is the cornerstone. (66)

As with many portions of the Gospel of Thomas, this passage has a verbal affinity with parts of the Gospels of Matthew, Mark and Luke. But there, as in relation to the previous verse, it is in relation to the rejection of Jesus as Messiah by the majority of the people of Israel. This, however, is quite different in its intention.

Basically Jesus is saying that what the world rejects God accepts, and what the world accepts, God rejects. That is a bit bald, but the principle is just that. Saint James wrote quite clearly: "Whosoever will be a friend of the world is the enemy of God" (James 4:4). And it works the other way, as well. In the Aquarian Gospel Jesus says that the more the world approves of someone, the less merit they truly have in the spirit. I have been observing this since my teen years. The liking or disliking of negative and ignorant people is an accurate index to the true character of those they like or dislike. What they dislike is good and what they like is harmful. That sounds very simplistic, and it is because those that Buddha calls "run-of-the-mill" are simplistic in most things. Though Yogananda rightly commented: "Human beings are skillful in their ignorance."

This is just about all that can be said. I could cite examples, but it would better if you considered your own experience and drew your own conclusions.

ALL–AND NOTHING

Jesus said, Whoever knows everything, but fails [to know] himself, lacks everything. (67–Brown translation)
Patterson and Maeyer: Those who know all, but are lacking in themselves, are utterly lacking.

Why are we here? Even more: why do we keep coming back here? The answer is that the creation is a vast school in which we must learn. Certainly we see that people have learned a great deal, much of it useless though certainly complex and the result of at least externalized intelligence. But back they come to this world over and over because they have not learned the "one thing needful" (Luke 10:42) and have not "chosen the good part" which is eternal. And that is the knowledge of who and what they are, a knowledge that will lead them to know God.

In the Bhagavad Gita we are told: "Know this [ultimate knowledge of the Self], and you shall not again fall into delusion. By this you shall come to see all creation in your Self and then in me. Even if you should be the most sinful among all the sinful, yet you would cross over all sin by the raft of knowledge alone. As the kindled fire reduces wood to ashes, in the same way the fire of knowledge reduces all karmas to ashes. No purifier equal to knowledge is found here in the world. He who is himself perfected in yoga in time finds knowledge in the Self" (Bhagavad Gita 4:35-38). He who possesses this knowledge has everything; without it he has nothing.

Jesus of course is not pointing us to mere intellectual knowledge, but to the knowing of the individual spirit that leads to the knowing of the infinite, cosmic Spirit. This is because in his years in India he had studied the Bhagavad Gita which had told him (and through him, us): "To you I shall explain in full this knowledge, along with realization, which being known, nothing further remains to be known in this world" (Bhagavad Gita 7:2). "To you I shall declare this most secret knowledge combined with realization, which having known you shall be free from evil" (Bhagavad Gita 9:1).

And now we have learned the same.

THE BLESSINGS OF PERSECUTION

Jesus said, Blessed are you when you are hated and persecuted. Wherever you have been persecuted they will find no place. (68)
> *Patterson and Maeyer:* No place will be found, wherever you have been persecuted.
>
> *Nancy Johnson:* They shall find no place still standing where they have tormented you.

It is well known to historians that the triumph of Christianity occurred because of the martyrdom of so many that "loved not their lives unto the death." In the book of Revelation we read: "I heard a loud voice saying in heaven, Now is come salvation, and strength, and the kingdom of our God, and the power of his Christ: for the accuser of our brethren is cast down, which accused them before our God day and night. And they overcame him by the blood of the Lamb, and by the word of their testimony; and they loved not their lives unto the death. Therefore rejoice, ye heavens, and ye that dwell in them" (Revelation 12:10-12).

Christianity is the only major world religion that from the beginning held out to its prospective converts the fact of their likely persecution and martyrdom. The enemies of Christianity have often remarked that they dared not create martyrs. No matter how greatly he wanted to kill Saint Tikhon, the Patriarch of Moscow, Lenin said: "We cannot afford a martyr." And today we see that the new martyrs of Russia have triumphed over their Communist persecutors. It is true that the blood of martyrs eventually annihilates those who have tormented them and often expunges the places of their suffering from the earth.

Jesus said, Blessed are they who have been persecuted within themselves. It is they who have truly come to know the father. Blessed are the hungry, for the belly of him who desires will be filled. (69)

Now Jesus expounds the martyrdom of the heart and spirit. Those that suffered inwardly and showed themselves willing to lay down their life for the faith are honored by the Eastern Christians especially, for they are considered martyrs of the spirit. Those who have offered their lives willingly, joyfully, have done more than conquer their enemies: they have drawn near to the Father and won a place in the holy kingdom. Those who hungered to sacrifice themselves because of love, and yearned for martyrdom have been glorified by what the Eastern Church calls "green martyrdom"–martyrdom without the shedding of blood (at least unto death). I have known several such martyrs in the Russian Orthodox Church and they were remarkable, possessing a spiritual power and quality that I saw in no one else. When they prayed, heaven heard and responded. Truly, whatever they asked they received because they only asked according to the highest will of God. May they pray for us all in that imperishable kingdom.

LIFE OR DEATH
LIE WITHIN

Jesus said, That which you have will save you if you bring it forth from yourselves. [But the lack of] that which you do not have within you will kill you if you do not have it within you. (70)

This is stated in a very uncompromising manner which is perfectly fitting because it is true that if a person brings forth divinity from within himself and possesses the transcendent experience and knowledge that bringing forth his inner reality entails, he—and he alone—shall be saved, liberated from the bondage of birth and death and all limitations forever. On the other hand, if he does not bring his immortal being forth, then that very lack will ensure his remaining in the realms of spiritual death.

"I call heaven and earth to record this day, that I have set before you life and death: therefore choose life, that thou mayest love the Lord thy God, and that thou mayest obey his voice, and that thou mayest cleave unto him: for he is thy life" (Deuteronomy 30:19-20).

ADMISSION

Jesus said, I shall destroy this house, and no one will be able to build it […]. (71)

There is simply no way to even feel slightly sure that I know what this means. So I will not fabricate something, but leave it alone.

NOT A DIVIDER

A man said to him, Tell my brothers to divide my father's possessions with me.

He said to him, O man, who has made me a divider?

He turned to his disciples and said to them, I am not a divider, am I? (72)

Often at the time of Jesus legal authorities would appoint a respected person whose honesty was accepted by all to decide on the apportionment of disputed properties. Jesus was not one of these, but a teacher of godliness instead of a meddler in the petty upsets of petty people (though it is a common trait of religious figures today).

In the Aquarian Gospel (111:4) Jesus says about this very subject of inheritance: "I am not come to be a judge in such affairs; I am no henchman of the court." So both these documents are consistent with one another.

SEEKING THE HARVEST

Jesus said, The harvest is great but the laborers are few. Beseech the Lord, therefore, to send out laborers to the harvest. (73)

This can have two meanings, outer and inner. The outer meaning is to ask for spiritual laborers to be sent into the world to call and instruct those who are inwardly ripe for harvest. The inner meaning is to ask abundant blessings and assistance either from God or his emissaries to uplift and purify us so the harvest of spiritual understanding can be reaped by us.

The implication is that both we and the world require assistance from God–either in the form of intuitional inspiration from God or intellectual awakening and teaching from those who have already gained the wisdom of God and have been sent to help us.

From that point on the harvesting is all up to us as evidence that we are worthy and capable aspirants.

THIRSTING IN VAIN

He said, O Lord, there are many around the drinking trough,
but there is nothing in the cistern. (74)

The book of Proverbs advises us: "Drink waters out of thine own cistern, and running waters out of thine own well" (Proverbs 5:15). But the prophet Jeremiah laments: "My people have committed two evils; they have forsaken me the fountain of living waters, and hewed them out cisterns, broken cisterns, that can hold no water" (Jeremiah 2:13).

The picture here is of many thirsting people crowding desperately around a drinking trough, but finding it dry because there is no water in the cistern itself, for the cistern is not whole or complete but is broken, so any water that might have entered the cistern will have drained away. No matter how much rainfall there may be, the cistern will be as dry as though it were in a desert. And the people will perish.

This is an apt symbol of a group of people that, however religious they might be, cannot survive spiritually because they have no inner spiritual resource upon which they can draw. There is no water of life in their souls. It is also a symbol of an individual who, having neglected to cultivate the interior life, is therefore incomplete and incapable of drawing upon any inner, spiritual reserves.

In the book of Revelation we find complete assurance that the water of life will be given to us abundantly. "I will give unto him that is athirst of the fountain of the water of life freely" (Revelation 21:6). "Whosoever will, let him take the water of life freely" (Revelation 22:17).

The water of life is given to all of us freely–at least potentially speaking. But two things are required of us: we must actively collect the water of life and we must retain it securely. This is done by dedicated and continual spiritual practice, especially meditation.

"Therefore with joy shall ye draw water out of the wells of salvation" (Isaiah 12:3).

WHO SHALL ENTER?

Jesus said, Many are standing at the door, but it is the solitary who will enter the bridal chamber. (75)

What is known as "bridal mysticism" is found in most spiritual traditions. The groom is the infinite Spirit and the bride is a finite spirit. Each one of us is to be wedded to God, but we must be faithful to our divine Bridegroom and be joined to none other. Ever. That is why Jesus (Matthew 19:4-5) taught that the prospective spouse must leave father, mother and all others behind and cling to their chosen one alone. "The solitary" Jesus refers to are those in whose hearts God alone can be found. They not only want no other, they refuse all others. Anyone not so dedicated is an adulterer in spirit.

Many are those who think they desire union with God. But only those who turn from everything else but God will find God. That is why Jesus said: "Many, I say unto you, will seek to enter in, and shall not be able" (Luke 13:24). Why? Because "the Lord looketh on the heart" (I Samuel 16:7) and sees that he is not the sole possessor. God neither gives nor receives that which is not all.

"And Jesus sat over against the treasury, and beheld how the people cast money into the treasury: and many that were rich cast in much. And there came a certain poor widow, and she threw in two mites, which make a farthing. And he called unto him his disciples, and saith unto them, Verily I say unto you, That this poor widow hath cast more in, than all they which have cast into the treasury: for all they did cast in of their abundance; but she of her want did cast in all that she had, even all her living" (Mark 12:41-44).

The foregoing is not just a pretty story. I knew a woman who told me virtually the same thing. Her father was dead and her mother made a living as a washerwoman. (This was in the early part of the twentieth century.) One Sunday when they went to church she and her sister knew that the three of them had nothing in the world but two quarters to live on for that week. When the collection was taken up, to their amazement their mother opened her purse. What was she going to do—actually give one of those quarters? No. *She took both quarters and put them in the collection plate.* The two girls were in shock. "But," Nellie told me, "the very next day some money came to us—more than fifty cents. And the two of us had learned a lesson we never forgot: God deserves everything we have."

As Sister Gyanamata, Yogananda's greatest disciple, said: God First. God Alone.

UNFAILING TREASURE

Jesus said, The kingdom of the father is like a merchant who had a consignment of merchandise and who discovered a pearl. That merchant was shrewd. He sold the merchandise and bought the pearl alone for himself. You too, seek his unfailing and enduring treasure where no moth comes near to devour and no worm destroys. (76)

The first thing this tells us is that the kingdom of heaven, the realm of infinite consciousness, is completely non-dual in character. It is not many, but only one: Satchidananda Brahman, the Absolute Unity.

To gain that kingdom we must "sell" or "trade in" all that is not the One. Such an endeavor requires us "spending" all we have to obtain the treasure. The widow of verse 75 gave all she had, and in this one the merchant spent all he had. The great poet-saint of India, Mirabai wrote a song in which she said: "I have sold everything in the market of this world and bought my Khanaiyya (Krishna). Some laugh and say the price was too high, and others say it was too low. But this I know: It was all I had."

To get the All we must give our all.

THE ALL SPEAKS

Jesus said, It is I who am the light which is above them all. It is I who am the all. From me did the all come forth, and unto me did the all extend. Split a piece of wood, and I am there. Lift up the stone, and you will find me there. (77)

As a rule great masters move among us as one of us, mostly concealing the vast difference between us and them so they can communicate wisdom to us. But occasionally they act and speak from their infinite side which is completely one with God. Their words are both their own and those of God since the Self of each one of us is part of God and participates in God's consciousness eventually.

It is I who am the light which is above them all. Everything is formed of Divine Light, but there is a Light of lights that transcends all those things. It is the transcendent Light that is "the True Light" spoken of by Saint John at the opening of his Gospel. We must realize that we, too, have this dual nature: immanent and transcendent.

It is I who am the all. From me did the all come forth, and unto me did the all extend. There is the potential All and the manifested All which came from it. There are two and yet really only one. The manifest All leads to the potential All; the relative leads to the absolute. They do not contradict one another, but are the essence of each other. Having one we have both, but it takes a great deal of development of consciousness to be able to intuit and then actually experience that.

Split a piece of wood, and I am there. Lift up the stone, and you will find me there. God is the inmost reality of every single thing. When by our mind refined by yoga we penetrate any thing or we look beyond its external appearance to the reality behind it, we will see God.

WELL-DRESSED
IGNORAMUSES

Jesus said, Why have you come out into the desert? To see a reed shaken by the wind? And to see a man clothed in fine garments like your kings and your great men? Upon them are the fine garments, and they are unable to discern the truth. (78)

In the Gospels of Matthew and Luke words similar to these are in reference to John the Baptist. However they could just as well be applied to Jesus himself.

The idea is not difficult to perceive. There is form and there is content. The outer appearance that pleases and attracts is almost always without any value, without any authentic spiritual content. In our modern world almost everything has become a matter of packaging. So much so that many people cannot see beyond the external appearance and remain enamored of valueless things that appear valuable. In religion this abnormality has become the norm. That which appeals to a barren mind will almost certainly itself be barren.

But Jesus implies a very important principle. A worthy spiritual teacher is one that can discern truth—and therefore falsehood as well.

Consequently we should give little attention to how any teacher looks, and no attention at all to what their followers say about them. We must scrutinize them and see if truth is known to them and imparted by them. But to do that, we must ourselves be capable of discerning the truth. And if that is true, then why not learn from ourselves? If it really does take one to know one, then all those who follow an incarnation of God (avatara) must themselves be incarnations of God.

What is the solution to this dilemma? We should not be seeking others, we should be seeking ourselves. That is, we should be yogis intent on the realization of the Self. As the light of the Self becomes visible to the yogi, so also do those who know the Self. By investigating inner realities it is possible to begin perceiving the reality of what is outside as well.

Therefore the answer to all problems is to become swayamprakash–self-illuminated. Otherwise, what good can any external factor be for us? We are the problem and we are the solution, not something outside us.

"Therefore, become a yogi" (Bhagavad Gita 6:46).

TRUE BLESSEDNESS

> A woman from the crowd said to him, Blessed is the womb
> which bore you and the breasts which nourished you.
>
> He said to her, Blessed are those who have heard the word
> of the father and have truly kept it. For there will be days when
> you will say, "Blessed are the wombs which has not conceived
> and the breasts which have not given milk." (79)

The woman's words were a common way of paying a compliment
to someone in that culture, but Jesus takes them very seriously: as
not worthy to be taken seriously, for it is also very common for people
who have not had children to be thought fortunate, especially in times
of great difficulty. But whatever the outer conditions might be, "those
who have heard the word of the father and have truly kept it" shall be
blessed and happy.

What is the word of the father? The call to return to the Divine Unity
from which we all have come and to which we are destined to return.
Those who not only hear the word but order their life in such a manner
that they can successfully make the blessed and happy return to the
Bosom of the Father (John 1:18), are those who truly keep it.

Many are those that hear the call and for a while turn toward God and draw near, yet in time lose the momentum and turn back to the illusory world and again wander to no worthy purpose. We often think of people "falling" spiritually, but most people simply fizzle out like a damp firecracker and that is the end of the matter for that lifetime.

Those who heed the exhortation: "give diligence to make your calling and election sure: for if ye do these things, ye shall never fall" (II Peter 1:10), and continue to "press toward the prize of the high calling of God in Christ Jesus" (Philippians 3:14), will find a blessedness and happiness undreamed of by those who know only the ways of this temporal world.

A DUPLICATION

Jesus said, He who has recognized the world has found the body, but he who has found the body is superior to the world. (80)

This is really the same as verse 56 and means the same.

BALANCING THE INNER
AND THE OUTER

Jesus said, Let him who has grown rich be king, and let him who possesses power renounce it. (81)

I would like to tell you something that contradicts a great deal of "spiritual" lore: "Simple souls" do not manage in spiritual life except in cute little stories for the childish at heart. To be a seeker for the Divine with the aspiration to become one with him/it, we must be capable and conversant with reality on many levels. I have met and even lived with saints and adept yogis, and none were "childlike" except in the opinions of worldlings who thought their directness and total lack of guile and cunning was a trait of children–which it is not as anyone who has dealt much with children knows. Lack of control and blurting out anything that has come to mind is certainly childish, and no saint possesses such traits. Let us not forget that Jesus counsels us to be "wise as serpents, and harmless as doves" (Matthew 10:16). That requires a maturity and insight that no child ever has.

One thing that the worthy aspirant needs is the understanding that the rules and ways of the spirit are almost never those of the world–especially of human society. Therefore spiritual life cannot be conducted on the assumptions of worldly life. Often it contradicts those assumptions. And this verse deals with the discrimination needed to bring order into the life of those who seek to transcend this world and its delusions.

Let him who has grown rich be king. (Patterson and Maeyer: "Let one who has become wealthy reign." Brown: "Let whoever is enriched become sovereign.").

We know that those who seek the inner kingdom have no interest in this world. Yet in the first chapter of Revelation Saint John the Apostle says that Jesus "hath made us kings and priests unto God and his Father" (Revelation 1:6). Obviously that kingship and priesthood has nothing to do with worldly positions, honors or privileges, but with the spirit, the inner person of those who seek the kingdom which Jesus has assured us is within (Luke 17:21).

Jesus stated very simply that eternal life is knowledge–jnana (John 17:3). And so had every great teacher of India before him, especially Shankara. By knowledge is meant "knowledge combined with realization" (Bhagavad Gita 9:1). In other words it is wisdom and insight coming from deep within each knower (jnani). Those who are rich in divine knowledge alone are masters of themselves. That is why Solomon said: "He that ruleth his spirit [is better] than he that taketh a city" (Proverbs 16:32).

The seeker after the celestial kingdom does not want political ruler-ship, but certainly seeks for self mastery so he can direct his life in such a way that he readily overcomes the karmic compulsions to rebirth and passes into higher worlds for the evolution that will culminate in his total spiritual liberation. Such are "the kings unto God," the true masters of the "everlasting kingdom" (II Peter 1:11).

Let him who possesses power renounce it. Having centered his attention and interest in the inner world, the yogi next renounces all power of the outer world, because many faculties open in the evolving person that if turned outward will enmesh him in the world and bind him tighter to the ever-turning wheel of birth and death. And if by any chance he has already been born with worldly power of any kind that, too, he ruthlessly cuts off and casts away. Wise kings and emperors have abandoned their thrones and occupied themselves with the inner conquest. Some did so openly and others such as Tsar Alexander I of Russia (Saint Theodore Kuzmich) mysteriously disappeared only to reappear as saints far from the world and ways of men.

Here Jesus has given us a clear rule: the interior should be cultivated and the exterior should be diminished and laid aside as much as possible. We must fully possess the inner kingdom and turn away completely from the ways of the outer realms. We must become powerful inside and seemingly powerless outside.

NEAR AND FAR

Jesus said, He who is near me is near the fire, and he who is far from me is far from the kingdom. (82)

Toward the end of the Syrian Jacobite Liturgy there is a blessing which begins: "You who are near and you who are far…." This is meant spiritually, and here Saint Thomas has recorded a saying of Jesus regarding it.

He who is near me is near the fire. Those who are one with God on occasion speak very plainly about their spiritual status and their effect on others. This often confuses people, but to speak only as ordinary pious human beings would be to confuse them even more.

A great master sometimes speaks as a devotee, a teacher and as the embodiment of God. Jesus being an avatara, an incarnation of infinite consciousness, was much more God than man. Therefore he often said the same thing his Father would say. This should not be surprising considering that he said: "I and my Father are one" (John 10:30).

In the Bible we find the statement: "Our God is a consuming fire" (Hebrews 12:29) in the sense that contact with God dissolves all that is not God, making us one with him. To be near Jesus is to be near the deifying Fire that is God. Actually, this can also be said of any avatara who has been sent into the world for the liberation of human beings. Such a sacred being is able to transmute the consciousness of those close to him. Therefore the wise stay near.

He who is far from me is far from the kingdom. Those who ignore or reject the divine incarnations by their own will distance themselves from the kingdom of God–and therefore from God himself. To meet an avatara is an incredible thing, both positive and negative, because a positive response can virtually ensure our liberation, and a negative response guarantees our continued separation from God.

What of those who have not met an avatara? They can become near to any avatara of history simply by studying his teachings and thoughtfully pondering them. And since such a liberated being is permanently so and shares in the omniscience and omnipresence of God, a seeker can pray to him as readily as to God. By studying the avatara's life as well as teachings it is possible to enter into very real spiritual contact with him. Then the aspirant will surely come near the kingdom and be enabled to enter it.

SEEING THE UNSEEABLE

Jesus said, The images are manifest to man, but the light in them remains concealed in the image of the light of the father. He will become manifest, but his image will remain concealed by his light. (83)

> *Patterson and Maeyer:* Images are visible to people, but the light within them is hidden in the image of the Father's light. He will be disclosed, but his image is hidden by his light.
>
> *Brown:* The images are manifest to mankind, and the Light which is within them is hidden. He shall reveal himself in the imagery of the Light of the Father—and (yet) his image is concealed by his Light.

If a person is not really grounded in the ways and beliefs of Eastern Orthodox Christianity, he is tremendously hindered in understanding Christianity itself. Contrary to popular (especially "ecumenical") opinion, Western and Eastern Christianity are profoundly divided. It is not just a matter of a few beliefs, but of many fundamental differences in belief and a profound difference in attitude and perspective. They are as different from one another as any two of the world's other major religions. In many ways Eastern Orthodox Christianity is far more akin to the other Eastern religions than it is to Western Christianity.

Few in the West seem to grasp this, including the Eastern Orthodox in the West.

One of the basic aspects of Eastern Christianity is what we may call Light Mysticism. In every form of Eastern Christianity, "Orthodox" or "Oriental," we find a large amount of Hymns of Light dealing with the nature of God as Light, particularly deifying Light in which the individual spirit is united with God and made a perfect imaging or reflection of the Divine. This process is known as theosis–deification. The doctrinal conclusion is simple and direct: God is Light (I John 1:5). Contrary to Western theology which declares that the light seen at the Transfiguration of Christ was merely a created energy, a kind of manufactured glory, Eastern Christians adamantly state that the light seen by the apostles was God himself. Therefore they refer to it as Uncreated Light–as, by the way, did the great English mystic Richard Rolle, despite official Western Scholastic theology to the contrary.

Ultimately everything is Light, as Saint Bernard of Clairvaux saw in mystic vision when West and East were not so divided in beliefs. As I pointed out in the commentary on verse 62, in original Christianity the highest mystical experience was the vision of Divine Light in which the mystic perceived his oneness with that Light. Having understood this, we are ready to analyze this verse.

Saint Paul tell us that God "only hath immortality, dwelling in the light which no man can approach unto; whom no man hath seen, nor can see" (I Timothy 6:16). This is in keeping with David's praise: "O Lord my God, thou art very great; thou art clothed with honour and majesty. Who coverest thyself with light as with a garment" (Psalms 104:1, 2). However, the statement that no human being can see God does not at all imply that no beings can see God–only human beings and those of lesser evolution. When we evolve beyond humanity to a higher status such as that of the great bodiless powers: Angels, Archangels, Thrones, Dominations, Princedoms, Virtues, Powers, Cherubim and Seraphim, then God will be seen. Yet Eastern Christianity tells us that when we see God we will learn that we cannot see him: we will be seeing the Unseen. Of course this is not comprehensible to our limited human minds, but the great mystics of all ages and traditions have told us the same. In mystic knowing we can know that God is Unknowable. That is what the medieval mystical classic *The Cloud of Unknowing* is all about.

In mystic vision it is possible to see the essential, highest nature of all things, their archetypal being, yet they will be in an incomprehensible manner veiled by the Divine Light which we will both see and not see. That is, the inner light of everything will be covered by God himself who is Light. How and why? *Because everything is God.* There will be nothing but God to either see or not see. God will be both manifested and revealed, but in a manner of knowing that is rooted in unity, not duality. So seeing and knowing will not be that of an object, but a Self-revealing impossible to any but those who have become organically one with God, who can truthfully say with Jesus: "He that hath seen me hath seen the Father" (John 14:9).

Seeing Your
Unknown Side

Jesus said, When you see your likeness, you rejoice. But when you see your images which came into being before you, and which neither die nor become manifest, how much you will have to bear! (84)

Patterson and Maeyer: When you see your likeness, you are happy. But when you see your images that came into being before you and that neither die nor become visible, how much you will have to bear!

Nancy Johnson: When you see your likeness, you are happy, but when you see your images rising before you without subsiding or approaching, how long can you stand that?

Brill: When you see your likeness, you rejoice; but when you see your images which came into being before you–they neither die nor are made manifest–how much will you bear?

I doubt if anybody absolutely knows what this verse means, but I do know a possible interpretation so I will share it with you.

We have all had millions of incarnations, beginning with an atom of hydrogen and ending with our last human life. In each of these we have had a form, a body, in which we lived. And when death expelled us from those bodies we entered the astral world and took on a form there, as well.

Sometimes in meditation we see those previous forms in differing degrees of clarity. At other times we feel their vibration or intuit them more than we actually see a form. But whichever it might be, for me it is a very peculiar experience and one that I do not much care for. At such times I do not try to banish the experience, but just sit and keep on meditating as usual. After a bit the impression fades away and that is that, though on occasion another form takes its place.

Why does this happen? Mostly because our inner mind is doing a kind of psychic housecleaning and is discarding deep subconscious impressions that no longer have relevance. At such times it is a sign of karma being dissolved on a subliminal level. On other occasions it is an indication of some deeply buried impulse or karma that is being manifested momentarily. (We can reap or dissolve our karma both in dreams and during meditation just as we do in our ordinary waking life.)

In a sense those forms are "ghosts" of our former lives that are wandering in our subconscious mind. If it was not beneficial to perceive them it would not happen in meditation, so we should calmly observe them. There is no denying that it is something at least mildly unsettling, so this verse speaks of "bearing" or "standing" it. That is certainly my experience. But the only correct response is to keep centered on meditation and remain indifferent to everything else. After all, meditation called the ghosts up and will exorcise them, too. That is why Jesus said: "In your patience possess ye your souls" (Luke 21:19). The word translated "souls" is psyche–our own mind. Such experiencing of the forms of previous lives is a means for us to become masters of our entire psychic nature. We do not have to enjoy it, but we should value and appreciate it.

Our Forefather Adam

Jesus said, Adam came into being from a great power and a great wealth, but he did not become worthy of you. For had he been worthy, he would not have experienced death. (85)

Just as an oak tree has an organic connection with the very first oak tree of its genealogy, in the same way we all have a living connection with our first human foreparent. Whether the human race has several foreparents or only one, by looking at our present situation we can see that they all ended up the same: undergoing death.

All the lifeforms in the universe are a result of evolution. Either the forms themselves evolved or the Creator Mothers, the Elohim, made those forms exactly for the embodiment of spirits of a vast range of evolutionary progress. However it may be, the first human being in this creation cycle has been given the designation: Adam. So to make things easier I am going to assume that we are all descendants of Adam.

To reach the evolutionary level of humanity is a tremendous accomplishment, the result of millions of births in millions of bodies, each one reflecting a rung of the evolutionary ladder as we slowly moved upward toward humanity. It was no small thing to master each form so we could move on to the next one. Therefore both Adam and we have "come into being from a great power and a great wealth." We have become what we are because of the divine impulse within each one of us. The power of God has carried us onward in the stream of our many lives. And the accomplishments made in so many births is a great wealth indeed. God has placed at our disposal all the powers of creation.

Glorious as this was, Adam failed in his initial birth in Paradise, the astral realm just one step up from the earth plane. Allowing delusion to grip his mind and heart he "died" to Paradise and fell back to the material world where he began to inhabit the physical human form God had mercifully provided for him and Eve (Genesis 3:21), a form subject to continual birth and death until enough evolution had been attained that he could again rise to Paradise. (See *Robe of Light*.)

According to a Hebrew book, the *Nishmath Chaim*, a writing contemporary with Jesus: "The sages of truth remark that [the name] Adam contains the initial letters of Adam, David, and Messiah; for after Adam sinned, his spirit passed into David, and the latter having also sinned, it passed into the Messiah" (Folio 152, column 2). Therefore the first Christians believed that Jesus was the reincarnation of Adam and David returned to earth to make atonement for his failure as Adam which plunged all humanity into the sentence of death through untold ages.

When it is said that Jesus "died for the sins of the world" we have to understand it in this perspective. He was paying a karmic debt, not dying as a blameless sacrifice in place of others so their sins would be freely and effortlessly forgiven as has been taught for centuries. And in doing so he became indeed a savior, a great siddha or master, truly an avatara, an incarnation of divine consciousness. This is his greatness; and to substitute the theological mythologies of exoteric Christianity regarding him is to deny and insult him. For the truth is always greater than fiction–even official religious fiction.

BLESSED HOMELESSNESS

Jesus said, The foxes have their holes and the birds have their nests, but the son of man has no place to lay his head and rest. (86)

Patterson and Maeyer: [Foxes have] their dens and birds have their nests, but human beings have no place to lay down and rest.

Foxes and birds have a long way to go in traversing the evolutionary ladder until they can step off into the angelic levels of existence. Human beings, however, are standing on the top rungs of their present evolution, and if they are awakened they are looking for the means to take that step and exchange earthly, material life for a life increasingly more and more in the spirit. This being so, there is no real home or resting place for those evolved enough to understand that they are not the body nor even the mind, but the spirit. So they say with Rumi:

Thus o'er the angels' world I wing my way
Onwards and upwards, unto boundless lights;
Then let me be as nought, for in my heart
Rings as a harp-song that we must return to Him.

Although we think of the dead when we say the words: "Rest in the Eternal grant unto them, O Lord: and let light perpetual shine upon them," it is a prayer for all questing human beings: a prayer for all the living; a prayer for Life. For the Eternal is the only Goal of all evolving consciousnesses.

DOUBLY WRETCHED

Jesus said, Wretched is the body that is dependent upon a body, and wretched is the soul that is dependent on these two. (87)

Brown: Wretched be the body which depends upon (another) body, and wretched be the soul which depends upon their being together.

It is made very clear in the Gospels that Jesus had two levels of teaching. One was for his disciples whose entire lives were going to be dedicated to the highest ideals of spiritual life and the other was for ordinary people whose capacity for understanding and interest in higher things was limited. To each the Lord Jesus gave the kind of teaching they could understand and follow. In the Gospel of Thomas we find the teachings meant for the disciples. Their principles and demands will naturally seem too stringent for the ordinary reader, but it should be kept in mind when reading this commentary that the teachings were not meant for everyone and should be considered in that light.

Whatever people might want to think, it is evident to any objective reader of Buddha's life and teachings that Buddha was a monk and a teacher of monks, that the Sangha was purely monastic and Buddhism is a religion for monastics. And if we look honestly at the life and teachings of Jesus we will find that the monastic life was the ideal of original Christianity. Until the middle of the twentieth century the Roman Catholic Church officially taught that the monastic life was "evangelical perfection"–the ideal of the Gospels. The Council of Trent even pronounced anathema against those who denied that monasticism was the highest form of Christian life. The Eastern Orthodox Church still holds (mostly in silence outside the monasteries) that all Christians are called to monastic life, but that Jesus made allowance for those not able to follow this ideal. "He said unto them, All men cannot receive this saying, save they to whom it is given. For there are some eunuchs, which were so born from their mother's womb: and there are some eunuchs, which were made eunuchs of men: and there be eunuchs, which have made themselves eunuchs for the kingdom of heaven's sake. *He that is able to receive it, let him receive it*" (Matthew 19:11-12).

This verse is absolutely an insistence on the single, celibate life. In India Jesus had learned the ideal of kaivalya: the need for absolute solitary independence in life if liberation–often called kaivalya-mukti–was to be attained. In Buddhism, especially Theravada, it is said that the human being suffers from being bound to the five skandhas and barely manages to attain Nirvana. If someone marries then they are bound to ten skandhas–their five and their spouse's five. When a child is born then they are bound to fifteen skandhas, and so it goes as more children are born. Beside that, simply being in a family–that of one's own and that of one's spouse–compounds the weight and number of skandhas. Therefore the expression for monastic life is often "homeless," "gone forth" or "left-home."

In this perspective we can understand why Jesus says: "Wretched is the body that is dependent upon a[nother's] body," for freedom and independence is rendered impossible by such dependence. And even more so: "wretched be the soul which depends upon their being together." Such dependence is enslavement, making freedom of body, mind and soul impossible. And it is usually expanded to other relationships and even to society, especially in the matter of conformity of thought and behavior. "Being one's own" man or woman becomes impossible. And so does being God's man or woman.

I grew up occasionally hearing sung at church:

> On the Jericho Road
>   there is room for just two–
> No more and no less:
>   just Jesus and you.

I got the idea even as a child.

ONWARD AND UPWARD

Jesus said, The angels and the prophets will come to you and give to you those things you (already) have. And you too, give them those things which you have, and say to yourselves, 'When will they come and take what is theirs?' (88)

Part of the cosmic order includes the existence of a hierarchy which watches over the evolution of those just beneath them on the evolutionary ladder. In this way they, too, evolve upward for even in the higher worlds the order is: "love thy neighbour as thyself" (Matthew 22:39). Human beings are meant to spiritually foster the plant and animal life as well as the general life sphere of the earth itself. In the same way the angels and saints are appointed to assist human beings in their spiritual development.

The angels and the prophets will come to you and give to you those things you (already) have. Those who resolve to lead the higher life immediately attract the attention of those angels and saints whose task it is to protect and guide those who truly desire ascension in consciousness. It is good if the aspirant is aware of this and prays to them frequently and is aware of their patronage that comes to those who ask for it. Learning about saints and angels is a vital part of the Christian's spiritual life, especially those of esoteric perspective, because the assistance of these holy beings can contribute tremendously to success in all spiritual endeavors.

Though they help us greatly, yet it is as Jesus says: they give us what is ours already, but of which we were not previously aware. For example, a person of esoteric bent may be so absorbed in metaphysical forces and practices that he forgets the great power of simple, heartfelt prayer to God and his saints and angels. That power is inherent in him, but he does not realize the magnitude of such a simple thing as prayer. So they inspire him to pray and his inner resources make it effective. In that way they give us what is ours already. Especially assuming that the Christian is one that has access to a full sacramental life, there is much of his inner resources that remain to be shown him by his sacred patrons. (See *The Yoga of the Sacraments*.)

And you too, give them those things which you have. By heeding and forming a bond of spiritual friendship with them we "give" them what we have.

And say to yourselves, When will they come and take what is theirs? If we are totally faithful in our cooperation with our blessed helpers, then the higher powers that are fully manifest in them will begin to arise in us, and we will become more like the saints and angels and begin to yearn for the time when, as Jesus promised, "they may receive you into everlasting habitations" (Luke 16:9) where we shall join their ranks and then in turn begin helping those remaining on earth in their journey to ascension to higher worlds so like Rumi we will be able to say: "Thus o'er the angels' world I wing my way onwards and upwards, unto boundless lights."

TWOFOLD LIFE

Jesus said, Why do you wash the outside of the cup? Do you not realize that he who made the inside is the same one who made the outside? (89)

It seems to be the curse of religion on this earth that no matter how abstract, metaphysical or spiritual the teachings of a great master may be, his supposed disciples set about immediately (usually even before his death) creating a completely external religion that neglects, conceals and even destroys inner, spiritual understanding and makes impossible a truly spiritual way of life that tends toward transcendence of the world.

Although he could certainly say the same thing to contemporary Christians, Jesus was addressing the Pharisees who were obsessed with ritual purity, interested only in outer purity while contentedly filled inwardly with impurity to such a degree that they even sought and obtained the death of Jesus while scrupulously maintaining their ritual purity. "Then led they Jesus from Caiaphas unto the hall of judgment: and it was early; and *they themselves went not into the judgment hall, lest they should be defiled*; but that they might eat the passover.... Then said Pilate unto them, Take ye him, and judge him according to your law. The Jews [Judeans] therefore said unto him, It is not lawful for us to put any man to death:... Pilate therefore went forth again, and saith unto them, Behold, I bring him forth to you, that ye may know that I find no fault in him.... When the chief priests therefore and officers saw him, they cried out, saying, Crucify him, crucify him. Pilate saith unto them, Take ye him, and crucify him: for I find no fault in him. The Jews answered him, We have a law, and by our law he ought to die, because he made himself the Son of God.... When Pilate therefore heard that saying, he brought Jesus forth, and sat down in the judgment seat in a place that is called the Pavement, but in the Hebrew, Gabbatha. And it was the preparation of the passover, and about the sixth hour: and he saith unto the Jews, Behold your King! But they cried out, Away with him, away with him, crucify him. Pilate saith unto them, Shall I crucify your King? The chief priests answered, We have no king but Caesar. Then delivered he him therefore unto them to be crucified. And they took Jesus, and led him away. And he bearing his cross went forth into a place called the place of a skull, which is called in the Hebrew Golgotha: where they crucified him" (John 18:28, 31; 19:4, 6, 7, 13-18). Here we see the ultimate madness of externalized, exoteric religion.

Everything in relative existence is dual on many levels. Most basic is the fact that everything is twofold, possessing an interior and an exterior. Therefore any spiritual system that is going to lead us to higher consciousness must deal with both aspects of our being. Otherwise it will be ineffectual and ultimately hypocritical and spiritually destructive to those who adhere to it.

Jesus' words make it clear that true spiritual life is one of continual purification. Enlightenment is an inherent characteristic of every sentient being, but that inner light is buried beneath the debris of karma and the ignorance that spawns karma. We must continually purify all our levels of existence, inner and outer, until all that blocks the light of the spirit is removed and our eternal nature shines forth unhindered. This reveals that evolution is a process of refining and clearing our consciousness as well as all our bodies, gross and subtle. The only process that directly and fully purifies the consciousness is yoga. It is not a matter of choice but of necessity: each person must in time become a yogi and persevere. Then certainly we will be received "into everlasting habitations" as Jesus promised in the previous verse.

THE YOKE OF CHRIST

Jesus said, Come unto me, for my yoke is easy and my lord-ship is mild, and you will find repose for yourselves. (90)

Patterson and Maeyer: Come to me, for my yoke is comfortable and my lordship is gentle, and you will find rest for yourselves.

Nancy Johnson: Come to me for my yoke is light, my rule is mild and you shall find repose.

In commenting on verse eighty-seven I pointed out that Jesus' teaching was on two levels: one for the totally committed and one for those whose very real limitations restricted what Jesus could teach or require of them. This verse is for the committed disciples, for anyone who has had any experience knows that what those dedicated love and consider a source of peace and happiness will be considered miserable and laborious by those not so dedicated. Those who are being called by Jesus are those whose development enables them to appreciate the path of purification that leads to expanding awareness and spiritual fulfillment.

In my life I have seen people miffed and complaining about very mild disciplines and requirements, but I have also see people happy and cheerfully expressing their gladness at learning of very stringent things necessary for continuing their progress in spiritual life. It was all a matter of experience and the resulting perspective.

Those who have entered the path to Christhood and experienced its value are not reluctant to take upon themselves the discipline and purification required, for they have already gained a depth of insight and experience of inner life that draws them onward to attain more.

When we move onward we leave a great deal behind. For some that is a loss because of their attachment to those things, and for others it is viewed as a freedom from hindrance. The path of yoga, for example, demands not just a great deal, it demands everything. Yoga is fundamentally an all-or-nothing matter. It all depends on what we really want out of life, what we think life really is.

"The kingdom of heaven is like unto treasure hid in a field; the which when a man hath found, he hideth, and for joy thereof goeth and selleth all that he hath, and buyeth that field. Again, the kingdom of heaven is like unto a merchant man, seeking goodly pearls: who, when he had found one pearl of great price, went and sold all that he had, and bought it" (Matthew 13:44-46).

This is a picture of one who has caught the heavenly vision and realized the true value of things. For joy the seeker gives all that he has because he knows he shall receive so much more in return. What he will receive he wants; and he no longer wants those things that he must abandon to attain the kingdom of heaven, the realm of limitless consciousness.

The yoke of Christ is easy to bear because of what it bestows, and the lordship of Christ is mild when the guaranteed gain is so vast. Beyond all the worlds and their contents that the questing soul must leave behind as it moves from level to level of ever-increasing consciousness, there is a rest, a peace of spirit that is worth all that had to be sacrificed to attain it. Giving up what is now seen to have been really nothing, the dauntless yogi has come to possess everything. Total fulfillment is the result.

"Therefore if any man be in Christ, he is a new creature: old things are passed away; behold, all things are become new" (II Corinthians 5:17). It is worth the price; indeed the price was nothing. That is the secret that the saints and masters have come to know. And which we should learn from them.

KNOWING THE
UNKNOWN

**They said to him, Tell us who you are so that we may believe
in you.**

**He said to them, You read the face of the sky and of the earth,
but you have not recognized the one who is before you, and you
do not know how to read this moment. (91)**

Brown: They say to him: Tell us who thou art, so that we may
believe in thee. He says to them: You scrutinize the face of the sky
and of the earth–yet you do not recognize Him who is facing you,
and you do not know to inquire of Him at this moment.

The disciples have not yet crossed over from mere intellectual assent
or belief to the realm of direct intuitional experience that is not
believing or accepting but *knowing*. Therefore they ask Jesus to define
himself. Jesus tells them that they are able to tell by the appearance of
earth and sky the coming changes in those material things, but they
are unable to perceive his nature which transcends them. They neither
know him, nor do they know how they should ask him about the way
to attain such knowledge.

In the Bhagavad Gita, Arjuna the yoga adept has more understanding, so he says to Krishna: "O Supreme Lord, I wish to behold your Ishwara Form, O Purushottama. If you think it is possible for me to see it, O Lord of Yogis, then show to me your eternal Self" (Bhagavad Gita 11:3-4). As a yogi Arjuna understands that what he desires is a matter of mystical experience far beyond the ordinary mind. That it must be a revelation bestowed on him. So Krishna replies: "You are not able to see me with your own eyes. I give to you the divine eye: behold my Ishwara Power" (Bhagavad Gita 11:8). Then Arjuna sees the divine universal form of Krishna through the spiritual will and power of Krishna.

In the Gospel of Matthew we find this: "When Jesus came into the coasts of Caesarea Philippi, he asked his disciples, saying, Whom do men say that I the Son of man am? And they said, Some say that thou art John the Baptist: some, Elias; and others, Jeremias, or one of the prophets. He saith unto them, But whom say ye that I am? And Simon Peter answered and said, Thou art the Christ, the Son of the living God. And Jesus answered and said unto him, Blessed art thou, Simon Barjona: for flesh and blood hath not revealed it unto thee, but my Father which is in heaven" (Matthew 16:13-17).

As seekers for higher consciousness and knowledge we must realize that they come to us directly from the Supreme Source, the transcendental Being of God.

ASKING AND HEARING

Jesus said, Seek and you will find. Yet, what you asked me about in former times and which I did not tell you then, now I do desire to tell, but you do not inquire after it. (92)

Nancy Johnson: Jesus said: Seek and you shall find. What you have asked me recently I did not tell you then. I want to tell you now, when you are not asking me.

This verse can be understood in two different ways depending on which of these translations is the basis.

The first meaning is that often in the beginning of spiritual life people are not just keen to learn, their intuition is waking up and they inquire after aspects that ordinary people would never even consider. But in time they become self-satisfied and settle down to a kind of lukewarm involvement that they find comfortable and without challenges. Then when they reach the point where their former inquiries can be answered since their understanding has deepened, they have long ago forgotten their questions and even their interest.

In the second chapter of Revelation Jesus speaks well of those in the church of Ephesus, but concludes by saying: "Nevertheless I have somewhat against thee, because thou hast left thy first love" (Revelation

2:4). It is not unusual for human beings to level or cool off from their initial fervor in spiritual life. But what is needed is for the temperature to keep climbing with no slackening whatsoever. The only remedy for this is regular and faithful spiritual study and practice–especially meditation.

The second meaning is that often a person reaches out to what is beyond him, his confidence actually being a symptom of his unreadiness. But when he has become centered in his spiritual practice and has learned patience, then he is able to comprehend what he sought before but was not matured enough to encompass at that time. It is a kind of Zen principle: only when we stop asking are we ready for the answers; only when we no longer desire something are we capable of possessing it wisely and to our benefit. In other words: if you want it you should not have it, and if you no longer want it then it should be yours. This is the way things are with the topsy-turvy mind when we begin serious spiritual pursuit. Perseverance is the key.

GIVE NOT...

[Jesus said,] **Do not give what is holy to dogs, lest they throw them on the dung-heap. Do not throw the pearls to swine, lest they [...] it [...]. (93)**

Nancy Johnson: Do not give the sacred to dogs, lest it be cast on the dung-heap. Do not cast pearls before swine, lest they destroy them.

Brill: Give not that which is holy to the dogs, lest they cast them on the dung-heap; cast not the pearls to the swine lest they grind them [to bits].

It is always a bit of a jolt to read of Jesus calling certain people dogs and pigs, but it is a worse jolt to see how many people merit those epithets!

A friend of mine told me of a great saint in Kashmir with whom he was acquainted. This saint would stand at the top of a small hill and large crowds would stand further down absorbing his holy vibrations in silence. One of the saint's devotees was the brother of Prime Minister Shastri. He was often disturbed by the saint's references to those who came to see him as "animals." Finally during one darshan session he worked up the courage to express his discomfort to the saint.

"Come here close to me," the saint ordered. He did so, and the saint touched him at the third eye, then told him to turn and look at the assembly. He did, and to his horror saw that nearly all of them had the heads of animals, including reptiles. As he stood there aghast, the saint quietly said to him: "This is how I always see them. According to their character so do I see them with different kind of animal heads. How many humans do you see here?" "Hardly any," replied Mr. Shastri. "That is because only a few out of all these people are really human in their hearts and minds. The rest are still subhuman."

From then on, the devotee felt sympathy for the saint who was trying to turn beasts into men.

Certainly we must respect all sentient beings, especially human beings because they bear the image of God—at least potentially. But we must respect holy things as well and not degrade them by giving them into the hands of those incapable of either understanding or valuing them. For if we do they shall incur the negative karma of disrespecting or even despising that which is holy and rejecting or even destroying the holy gifts. And in so doing they will harm themselves, not that which is holy. The ignorant often have to be protected from themselves. We, too, must be cautious lest we handle sacred things carelessly by giving them into the hands of the uncomprehending and thereby create negative karma for ourselves as well.

SEEKING AND KNOCKING

Jesus said, He who seeks will find, and he who knocks will be let in. (94)

This is not a "precious promise" as exoteric Christians think, but the enunciation of an irrevocable law. For seeking and knocking are actions that by the nature of things will provoke a response. Our lives are totally in our hands; we shape them according to our thoughts and deeds. Seeking will result in finding and knocking will result in entering. So we had better be sure that we really want what we seek and that we want to end up where we have knocked. And we must be sure beforehand what will be the exact reaction to our seeking and knocking. If we know what we are about we can make our life glorious. If we do not know, then our life will be confused and a misery. We truly do make either heaven or hell right here on earth. This is the power wielded by every human being to either ill or good.

RIGHT GENEROSITY

Jesus said, If you have money, do not lend it at interest, but give it to one from whom you will not get it back. (95)

This is certainly noble advice, but it is much more practical and advantageous than noble. If you have money and lend it at interest the interest received is the only karmic reaction or reward. But if you give money to someone who cannot pay it back you will create the positive karma of being helped without demand of repayment by others when your karma brings you into times of destitution. So you are investing in the future. This is a lesson few learn because they want to grasp what is right in front of them at the time without regard to future possibilities. As in the previous verse the tremendous power we wield through intelligent understanding and employment of the law of karma is being shown us.

THE EXPANDING
KINGDOM

**Jesus said, The kingdom of the father is like a certain woman.
She took a little leaven, concealed it in some dough, and made
it into large loaves. Let him who has ears hear. (96)**

The kingdom of the father referred to in this verse is the evolving
cosmos. The leaven spoken about is the karmic and evolutionary
force inherent in the energy structure of the universe itself. At the heart
of everything is the divine nature whose purpose is its own revelation.
This is the leaven that works from within to without with the intention
of revealing itself. Until that revealing it is hidden and there is no hint
of its presence. Furthermore that revealing is intended to come about in
an exact order and culminate in the same way that the tree results from
a seed. The patterns of this revelation are held in the consciousness of
God, since the cosmos itself is the incarnation of God. It is the innate
divine nature of all things that is the force impelling them toward the
heights of evolution and the revelation of their divinity. The kingdom of
the father is the dream of the father, and its perfection is the awakening
in which all participate ultimately.

THE FULFILLED UNIVERSE

This ninety-seventh verse of the Gospel of Thomas continues the theme of the universe and its evolution. It is related to the 129th hymn of the 10th Mandala of the Rig Veda that has come to be known as the Nasadiya Shukta. Here is T. H. Griffith's translation:

1. Then was not non-existent nor existent: there was no realm of air, no sky beyond it. What covered it, and where? and what gave shelter? Was water there, unfathomed depth of water?
2. Death was not then, nor was there aught immortal: no sign was there, the day's and night's divider. That One Thing, breathless, breathed by its own nature: apart from it was nothing whatsoever.
3. Darkness there was: at first concealed in darkness this All was indiscriminated chaos. All that existed then was void and formless: by the great power of Warmth was born that Unit.
4. Thereafter rose Desire in the beginning, Desire, the primal seed and germ of Spirit. Sages who searched with their heart's thought discovered the existent's kinship in the non-existent.
5. Transversely was their severing line extended: what was above it then, and what below it? There were begetters, there were mighty forces, free action here and energy up yonder.

6. Who verily knows and who can here declare it, whence it was born and whence comes this creation? The Gods are later than this world's production. Who knows then whence it first came into being?

7. He, the first origin of this creation, whether he formed it all or did not form it, Whose eye controls this world in highest heaven, he verily knows it, or perhaps he knows not.

Now we should look at the verse itself.

Jesus said, The kingdom of the father is like a certain woman who was carrying a jar full of meal. While she was walking on the road, still some distance from home, the handle of the jar broke and the meal emptied out behind her on the road. She did not realize it; she had noticed no accident. When she reached her house, she set the jar down and found it empty. (97)

The jar is the cosmos and the meal is all that the cosmos contains in potential–and eventually actualized–form. At first there is no overt manifestation, but only a steady expansion which eventually results in the emergence of evolving forms. From that point on the drama of creation is carried out. That is why this verse says that the woman walked for a while on the road before the meal emerged and began falling on the road. In her experience there was no differentiation between the first half of the journey in which no meal appeared and the second half where the trail was laid out along the road as the jar emptied itself. The woman's not noticing all this is a symbol of the spontaneous nature of emerging and withdrawing creation. It makes no difference to the "carrier" of the universe.

The complete emptying of the jar and the arrival at home were simultaneous. That is, when the creative will inherent in the universe was expended, the creative process was completed.

No simile is perfect, and this one certainly is not. The Veda is not saying that creation takes place in a totally unconscious manner. Actually the creation is fully conscious, being a manifestation of the Infinite Consciousness. What it does mean, however, is that creation is a continuous process, seamless from beginning to end. To an outside observer it may appear to be progressing in stages, but in reality it is a single movement activated by a single will.

The seventh verse: "He, the first origin of this creation, whether he formed it all or did not form it, whose eye controls this world in highest heaven, he verily knows it, or perhaps he knows not" is not implying that God is unaware of the creation as his activity. What it does mean is that God has not planned out or worked out the creation in the manner that a human being would plan and carry out a project. There is nothing intellectual in the process, because God does not possess a mind. In the perfect knowing that is the very nature of God, the creation comes forth and is withdrawn in the same eternal, timeless moment. In a sense the creation has no past, or present or future. It is a single thing, as is its Creator.

When a motion picture is shown in a theater, it appears to begin, proceed and end, taking up a certain amount of time. But this is illusory. Even before the showing the entire thing is present in its container. It takes time to project, but its contents are always present simultaneously. So although the audience sees something taking place, the only thing that is happening is the audience's perception of it. It takes up time, and it takes up space, but it is really beyond time or space. It is the same with creation.

What is the exact message of this verse? Do not get caught in the illusion. Step back and see it as it is: simply Light projected on Light. And you yourself are that Light.

Taking Stock

Jesus said, The kingdom of the father is like a certain man who wanted to kill a powerful man. In his own house he drew his sword and stuck it into the wall in order to find out whether his hand could carry through. Then he slew the powerful man. (98)

Brill: The kingdom of the Father is like a man who wanted to kill a great man. He drew the sword in his house and drove it into the wall, that he might know that his hand would be strong. Then he slew the great man.

In the Gospel of Luke we find this parallel passage: "Which of you, intending to build a tower, sitteth not down first, and counteth the cost, whether he have sufficient to finish it? Lest haply, after he hath laid the foundation, and is not able to finish it, all that behold it begin to mock him, saying, This man began to build, and was not able to finish. Or what king, going to make war against another king, sitteth not down first, and consulteth whether he be able with ten thousand to meet him that cometh against him with twenty thousand? Or else, while the other is yet a great way off, he sendeth an ambassage, and desireth conditions of peace" (Luke 14:28-32).

It is as good to know what we cannot do as it is to accurately know what we can do. I have not seen this principle honored much throughout my life. Quite the opposite is true: it is considered right to boast and swagger and believe that nothing is impossible for a person. As a child I encountered this, and as an adult was astounded when I saw the contempt that would be shown toward anyone who dared to say that their abilities were limited. Childish egotism apparently is favored by most people as a substitute for ability and success.

However that may be, Jesus does not hold the majority view. So he tells us that in spiritual life we must be tested and proved—mostly by ourselves—just like the man in this parable. He put himself to the test and when he succeeded he went out and destroyed his enemy. In spiritual life we must be strong and endurant to overcome those forces within and without that hinder us from raising our consciousness and mastering life rather than being mastered by it.

Spiritual ambition is of no consequence whatsoever if there are no inner resources to support it. Therefore the spiritual aspirant must consider well the obstacles and opposition he must overcome and make himself strong and capable for the struggle. Cultivation of his inner resources through spiritual disciplines and meditation is essential for success. Only those sufficiently disciplined and adept in yoga—those who have first set their own house in order—can hope to be victorious in what is a very real battle against the giants of ignorance and illusion.

THE SPIRITUAL FAMILY

**The disciples said to him, Your brothers and your mother
are standing outside.**

**He said to them, Those here who do the will of my father
are my brothers and my mother. It is they who will enter the
kingdom of my father. (99)**

Before beginning an analysis of this verse I would like to point out
that "brothers" do not necessarily mean children of one's mother,
but also cousins. This is still the situation in India. Having met the only
brother of a good friend of mine, I was bewildered when my friend kept
introducing me to men, saying: "This is my brother." When after about
half a dozen of these introductions I said that I thought he had only one
brother, he answered: "Yes. But these are my cousin-brothers!" Then I
got the idea. Actually, I have been amazed at how much a few visits to
India can clarify many aspects of Jesus' life of two thousand years ago.

"If any man be in Christ, he is a new creature: old things are
passed away; behold, all things are become new" (II Corinthians
5:17). "And I saw a new heaven and a new earth: for the first heaven
and the first earth were passed away; and there was no more sea"
(Revelation 21:1). "And he that sat upon the throne said, Behold, I

make all things new" (Revelation 21:5). When someone begins living an authentic spiritual life, everything begins to change. Even while in this world, the sea of samsara begins to evaporate for him. If this does not happen, then the new life in the spirit has not begun and something is seriously wrong.

"And be not conformed to this world: but be ye transformed by the renewing of your mind, that ye may prove what is that good, and acceptable, and perfect, will of God" (Romans 12:2). Part of the renewing process is the acquisition of a spiritual family, of spiritual friends. This is a very important part of spiritual life, and frankly if you live in an area where you cannot find such new relations, then please seriously consider moving to another place altogether.

Yogananda often said: "Company is stronger than will power." Satsanga, company with seekers of God, is an essential factor in spiritual life, and often means the difference between perseverance and failure. This I have seen throughout the more than fifty years of being a yogi. In fact, as soon as I learned about yoga I began making arrangements to move halfway across the country so I could be with other yogis and learn from them. That was one of the most sensible things I have ever done. Every day I lived in close personal contact with yogis who meant business, many of whom had lived for years with Paramhansa Yogananda. Those years were truly the happiest and most blessed of my life.

We have a close relation with our parents and family and often owe them a great deal, but when the path of light opens before us we should realize that there is a much more significant family for us to join: the company of devotees of God. Those who live for God and seek to enter the kingdom of his boundless light and life are our real family. Hopefully we will no longer be coming back to this world and earthly birth and family, but will step up to the next rung on the ladder and live with those who have sought and found, knocked and opened. They are those that will be with us all the way to liberation in Spirit. Jesus knew this, and so should we.

THREE DEBTS

They showed Jesus a gold coin and said to him, Caesar's men demand taxes from us.

He said to them, Give Caesar what belongs to Caesar, give God what belongs to God, and give me what is mine. (100)

As spiritual aspirants we owe a great debt to three sources.

The first is to all those persons and things in the world which have fostered and benefitted our material life. "Caesar" includes all who have benefitted us, beginning with our parents and family, and all society and especially our friends. They are listed first because material awareness is the first center of the human being's life. To "Caesar" we owe respect, cooperation and even on occasion personal sacrifice. Part of our duty is to remember this at all times.

The second debt is to God, the awareness of whom arises as we develop and evolve. To God we owe reverence, worship and obedience to divine law. This takes precedence over the first debt, and if there is ever a conflict between the two it should be resolved by putting God first and acting accordingly.

The third is to our spiritual teachers, to whom we owe much the same that we owe God, though to a lesser degree. This, debt, too, must always be secondary to the debt to God. I point this out because there is no place in spiritual life for the fanatical and slavish attitudes often projected toward spiritual authorities, including unquestioning acceptance and obedience. To spiritual teachers and their teachings we owe respect, attention, intelligent application and devotion–but only to a degree that is beneficial to us and sensible. Again, fanaticism and slavery do not enter into our debt to God, much less to the godly.

We could sum it all up by saying that our debt to others and society is to live as wisely, worthily and helpfully as possible. Our debt to God is to live as spiritually devoted as possible, and that includes observance of authentic spiritual disciplines and practices which bring us closer to the Divine. Our debt to spiritual teachers is to act in conformity with their wisdom and ourselves become wise and help others in turn. It is all very simple, but requires a lifetime to repay all three debts.

FATHER AND MOTHER

[Jesus said,] Whoever does not hate his father and his mother as I do cannot become a disciple to me. And whoever does not love his father and his mother as I do cannot become a disciple to me. For my mother […], but my true mother gave me life. (101)

Nancy Johnson: He who does not hate his father and his mother as I do cannot be my disciple, and who does not love his mother and father as I do, cannot be my disciple. For my mother killed me, but my true mother has given me life.

Brown: Whoever does not hate his father and his mother in my way, shall not be able to become a Disciple to me. And whoever does [not] love his [Father] and his Mother in my way, shall not be able to become a Disciple to me. For my mother [bore me], yet [my] true [Mother] gave me life.

This verse clearly implies that each of us has two sets of "parents"–one false and one true. One is to be despised or disregarded, and the other is to be loved and clung to. We, too, are dual, having a false nature and a true nature–one of which we should disregard and one of which we should hold to. Our two natures are material and spiritual. In the Bible there are statements about the sins of the fathers being visited on the children unto the third and fourth generations. This is really about the karma created in our previous bodies that are in a sense the "fathers" of our present body. Actually the incarnate human is subject to two forces: those of the body and those of the mind. These correspond to Adam and Eve in the private history of each of us. So our previous bodies are our fathers and our previous minds are our mothers. Both have produced the karma we are reaping.

Those who have attained a spiritual, intuitive perspective realize that we have two spiritual parents: God the Father and God the Mother. Our Father is eternal Spirit and our Mother is eternal Power that embodies itself in creation and moves us along the evolutionary path from life to life. The Father sends us forth into the evolutionary womb of the Mother who fosters us and unerringly brings us to the perfect status of Sons of God, thus completing the triune nature of eternal existence.

Therefore we should disregard and turn from the material temporal parents–our body and mind–for this is what the word translated "hate" really means. And we should love our eternal Father and Mother. Our false mother gave us material birth which ended always in death, but our Divine Mother has given us ever-expanding life in the form of evolving spiritual consciousness. Therefore Nancy Johnson's translation says that one mother killed us and the other gave us life.

There is a saying in India: "The parents give birth; but God gives life. There is an end to birth; there is no end to life." So everyone turns from one set of parents and holds fast to the other. Some choose death and some choose life. The choice is ours.

EXOTERIC RELIGION

Jesus said, Woe to the pharisees, for they are like a dog sleeping in the manger of oxen, for neither does he eat nor does he let the oxen eat. (102)

In the Gospel of Matthew we read: "Woe unto you, scribes and Pharisees, hypocrites! for ye shut up the kingdom of heaven against men: for ye neither go in yourselves, neither suffer ye them that are entering to go in" (Matthew 23:13). This is what Jesus is referring to in this verse. The entire focus of the Pharisees was on the letter of the law. Their righteousness was totally external, even to the extent of calculating how deep in the water the hands had to be immersed before they could be declared to be truly washed. The Pharisees are representative of exoteric religion, whatever the tradition. Obsessed with material observance they completely neglect the truly spiritual. No country or religion is free from this type of person. The most extreme examples I have seen have been in India, actually. They were rare, but their rarity made them all the more preposterous.

Exoteric religion keeps pointing their members to the material and away from the genuinely spiritual (which they often denounce as false or evil). Thus they give them a thoroughly material, external religious life and blind them to the spiritual, internal religious life that is true religion. Inimical to the Spirit they recreate their members in their own image. Therefore Jesus further said: "Woe unto you, scribes and Pharisees, hypocrites! for ye compass sea and land to make one proselyte, and when he is made, ye make him twofold more the child of hell than yourselves" (Matthew 23:15). The word translated "hell" is actually Gehenna, the Valley of Hinnom, the garbage dump of Jerusalem where fires smoldered perpetually and the maggots kept right on living and multiplying. Certainly Gehenna was a symbol of negative astral worlds, but it is also a symbol of this world of samsara, the realm of constant rebirth and death and their attendant and inevitable suffering.

Exoteric religion is not just the gate of hell (Gehenna), it is hell itself.

READY FOR INVASION

Jesus said, Fortunate is the man who knows where the brigands will enter, so that he may get up, muster his domain, and arm himself before they invade. (103)

Patterson and Maeyer: Congratulations to those who know where the rebels are going to attack. [They] can get going, collect their imperial resources, and be prepared before the rebels arrive.

Brown: Blest be the person who knows in [which] part the bandits may invade, so that he shall arise and collect his [things] and gird up his loins before they enter.

The universe being dual in nature, we must realize that there are elements that will help us move upward in evolution and elements that will send us downward in the opposite direction. These are the brigands, rebels or bandits spoken of in this verse in the three translations. Sometimes they are merely energy fields, sometimes other human beings, and sometimes objects and situations that impel our minds downward. We must protect ourselves from their invasion. And that requires us to rouse ourselves up to awareness and preventive action.

The first step is to know where they invade: the body, mind, senses or other unguarded aspects of our being and life. We must understand the strategy of the enemy as well as the weakness of our "fortress"–our entire body-mind complex. Then we must strengthen those areas so they cannot be broken down. Often we need to plug up possible entryways by making strong the areas that have become weakened or damaged by neglect or wrong thought and action.

The second step is to collect our scattered attention, energies and resources and have them under our command, obedient to our higher will so they cannot be stolen away from us and turned against us.

The third step is to prepare and arm ourselves with both the knowledge, the strategies and the power (strength) to defend ourselves. Foremost in all this is the knowledge and practice of yoga meditation.

Those who follow these three steps diligently will indeed be fortunate and blessed.

PENITENTIAL DISCIPLINE, ANYONE?

They said to Jesus, Come, let us pray today and let us fast.
Jesus said, What is the sin that I have committed, or wherein
have I been defeated? But when the bridegroom leaves the bridal
chamber, then let them fast and pray. (104)

There are certain people who have a pathological attachment to practices of self-denial, especially those that cause them discomfort. Usually this attachment is based on self-loathing and a masochistic desire for punishment. At the same time it is a way to continually draw attention to themselves. Fasting is for some reason an obsession with many, especially if it gives them a chance to publicly refuse food and tell others that they are fasting. Others of this type are continually observing silence in public where they can make a point of it to everyone. Both of these not only make themselves the center of attention, they manage to make everyone around them feel awkward and embarrassed, unsure of how to respond and act. If they can also manage to inconvenience others, it is an added bonus. Their fasting and silence are never done in private with no one else knowing about it. They are spiritual sociopaths.

Jesus has just been invited by these neurotic exhibitionists to join them in holy self-denial. He immediately and vehemently rejects the proposal on the ground that it has no purpose; that indeed such observances may have relevance when there is need of self-purification, but otherwise are pointless displays.

There are other forms of this peculiarity, almost always involved with food for some reason. The perpetrators like to refuse something offered them and ask for something peculiar and hopefully difficult to supply. (In *The Screwtape Letters* one of them asks for weak tea and dry toast, as I recall.) Here, too, we are dealing with a kind of Pharisee who makes a big to do so everyone knows how disciplined and self-denying they are.

Having said all that, I must add that Jesus indicates there are times when such discipline is appropriate, but only when done in private and for good (right) reasons. And he has shown us how to deal with such people. I hope you keep it in mind.

DARING TO KNOW

Jesus said, He who knows the father and the mother will be called the son of a harlot. (105)

> *Nancy Johnson:* He who knows his father and his mother shall be called a bastard.
>
> *Brown:* Whoever acknowledges father and mother, shall be called the son of a harlot.

People who love lies hate truth and people who love illusion hate reality and denounce both as lies and illusions. If we have not figured that out we are poorly equipped to get through this world. Anyone who dares seek God incurs the wrath of the children of satanic delusion. Consequently the enemies of Jesus had three lies they diligently propagated about him: 1) He was illegitimate ("We be not born of fornication" John 8:41). 2) He was a Samaritan ("Say we not well that thou art a Samaritan?" John 8:48). 3) He was possessed by a demon ("Thou hast a devil" John 7:20; 8:52; 10:20).

He told his disciples: "It is enough for the disciple that he be as his master, and the servant as his lord. If they have called the master of the house Beelzebub, how much more shall they call them of his household?" (Matthew 10:25). And so they will.

I knew a Franciscan friar whose whole life was service to others. Every day he took food to the hungry, and as he went the children of the devil called after him: "Hey Jim Jones!" More than one spiritual teacher of my acquaintance was called "a modern-day Rasputin."

As the Scots so wisely declare: "'They' have 'said,' and 'they' will 'say.' So let them be saying!"

ENDING DUALITY

Jesus said, When you make the two one, you will become the sons of man, and when you say, 'Mountain, move away,' it will move away. (106)

Making the two one

Unity is always the state of everything: duality is only part of the dream aspect of relative existence, of creation. So what Jesus is saying is that we must dispel the illusion of duality–banish it from our mind–not by intellectual affirmation or any thought process but by entering into the state of Oneness though meditational experience, through prolonged practice of yoga. This is possible because unity lies at the very heart of our existence; it is our eternal nature.

Becoming the Sons of Man

Jesus often referred to himself as Son of Man, and the expression occurs over eighty times in the four Gospels. It appears even more times than that in the Old Testament where it is used by God and angels to address prophets and others that are being taught by direct revelation. So just as Jesus is not *the* Christ, but rather *a* Christ, in the way he was a Son of Man in the sense that all human beings are destined to be just the same as he.

Sons of Man and Sons of God are really the same thing, which is reasonable considering that man and God are one. That being so, these words of Saint Paul are very significant for us: "The earnest expectation of the creation waiteth for the manifestation of the sons of God.... Because the creation itself also shall be delivered from the bondage of corruption into the glorious liberty of the children of God. For we know that the whole creation groaneth and travaileth in pain together until now" (Romans 8:19, 21, 22). Creation itself is the great womb of God in which all sentient being are gestating (evolving) unto the point of delivery (birth) into the Infinite Consciousness as liberated Sons of God.

Moving the mountain

The mountain will move when the Sons of God tell it to, because they are one with the mountain. In this verse, as well as in similar ones in the Bible, a mountain is any obstacle to spiritual life and progress. It is literal, too, because I have seen Dur Mountain in Cairo which moved several miles at the command of a Coptic Orthodox saint, a simple shoemaker. (After it had moved some miles he called out: "Dur!" which means "Stop!" So it is called Dur Mountain.) Anyone can see from the strata of the mountain that it is sitting in a place not native to it. If you go to its point of origin you see that the strata fit perfectly like pieces of a puzzle. No geologist can honestly deny the fact that the mountain is now sitting miles from its original location.

The vistas opened to us by Jesus have no boundaries except those we set ourselves.

"I Love You More..."

> Jesus said, The kingdom is like a shepherd who had a hundred sheep. One of them, the largest, went astray. He left the ninety-nine sheep and looked for that one until he found it. When he had gone to such trouble, he said to the sheep, "I care for you more than the ninety-nine." (107)
>
> *Nancy Johnson:* The kingdom is like a shepherd, who owned a hundred sheep, the largest of which went astray. He left the ninety-nine, in search of the one until he found it. After all his trouble, he said to the sheep: I love you more than the ninety-nine.

The amazing message of this verse is the fact that rather than being the trap ignorant human beings have made of it, the entire forces of the cosmos are on our side and working for our freedom. For this verse is not about Jesus or God, but about "the kingdom" which in this case means the entire evolutionary "mechanism" that is creation. So "I care for you more than the ninety-nine" is not a personal matter, but a statement that the entire cosmos has been set in motion to bring the straying souls back to the Bosom of the Father. Obviously the cosmos has very little interest in those that are safely home with the Father, having successfully traversed the evolutionary range and attained liberation. In fact, the universe is no longer relevant to them unless they choose to return to help others that are still wandering in confusion.

As a footnote, you might be interested to know that the Eastern Christian Churches, Orthodox and Oriental, believe in life on other planets, as Christianity did from the beginning. It is their belief that the parable of the lost sheep found in the Gospels of Matthew (18:12-13) and Luke (15:4-7) is not about an individual, but about the planet earth specifically. They teach that only the human beings on earth have fallen and gone astray through the malice of a fallen archangel. Therefore only the earth has needed a means for restoration and eventual liberation. This is just one point in which the Eastern Church is vastly more sophisticated than the Christianity of the West.

AT THE SOURCE

Jesus said, He who will drink from my mouth will become like me. I myself shall become he, and the things that are hidden will be revealed to him. (108)

I have already pointed out that liberated masters often speak on two very different levels: from their finite spirit and from the infinite Spirit with which they are one. Consequently they sometimes speak as God and sometimes as only themselves, which can be confusing to those who do not possess a more metaphysical understanding. Naturally someone commenting on a master's words will have to decide which aspect is speaking, the finite or the infinite, and comment accordingly. It seems safest to me to consider this verse the words of the universal Christ or Christ Consciousness, the Only Begotten of the Father–the Son of God, the personal aspect of the Absolute "incarnate" within the body of the universe.

For many years Paramhansa Yogananda wrote a commentary on the Gospels which appeared in his magazine. Toward the end of his life he told some of his disciples that he had prayed to Jesus, asking him if he had correctly relayed his teachings through his articles. Jesus appeared to him and said: "The cup from which I drink, thou dost drink." Jesus drank from the mouth of the Father, and so did Yogananda.

The mouth of Jesus and the mouth of the Father are the same. Therefore, whatever the tradition of a master might be, his words will be the words of a Christ, a perfect son of God. As Yogananda also said, there is no real spiritual difference between the masters, for they are perfect reflections of the one and only God. That is why in his autobiography he speaks of "the Yogi-Christs of India." In chapter twenty-four he wrote: "Yoga has produced, in every age of India, men who became truly free, truly Yogi-Christs." Though not born in India, Jesus, too, was a Yogi-Christ of India where he lived more than half his life before beginning his mission to Israel and to which he returned after three years to live out the rest of his life. And those who "drink from his mouth" will be Yogi-Christs as well, one with God, one with the Cosmic Christ and one with all the Christs that have walked the earth.

Saint Paul, a Christ himself so identified with Jesus Christ that he even bore in his body the wounds of Jesus (Galatians 6:17), wrote: "We speak the wisdom of God in a mystery, even the hidden wisdom, which God ordained before the world unto our glory: which none of the princes of this world knew:… but God hath revealed them unto us by his Spirit: for the Spirit searcheth all things, yea, the deep things of God…. For who hath known the mind of the Lord, that he may instruct him? But we have the mind of Christ" (I Corinthians 2:7-8, 10, 16). This is indeed the state of a Christ, the state for which each one of us is destined. All we need is the Christ Yoga for our transformation.

FINDING THE
HIDDEN TREASURE

Jesus said, The kingdom is like a man who had a hidden treasure in his field without knowing it. And after he died, he left it to his son. The son did not know (about the treasure). He inherited the field and sold it. And the one who bought it went plowing and found the treasure. He began to lend money at interest to whomever he wished. (109)

This is an allegory of a person's awakening to the divine consciousness inherent in each one of us. The three people in the story are really incarnations of a single person and should be understood accordingly. In the Bhagavad Gita the thirteenth chapter is entitled: The Field and Its Knower. The body is said to be the field and the Self is its knower, or rather "the knower in the field." For the Self is the hidden treasure.

The kingdom is like a man who had a hidden treasure in his field without knowing it. And after he died, he left it to his son. The son did not know (about the treasure). He inherited the field and sold it.

For many incarnations we have no idea of the Self. We may believe that there is an immortal part or "something" to us, but a comprehension of the Self is completely absent from our minds. So we keep passing on the subtle bodies which make up the field from incarnation to incarnation, to our various reincarnations–our "descendants." Often knowledge from our past lives exists to be carried over as a subconscious knowledge in each incarnation.

And the one who bought it went plowing and found the treasure. Finally in one incarnation we decide to "buy" the field. That is, we decide to control it, understand its purpose, master it and bring some order and even happiness and fulfillment into our life. Our motivation may not be completely spiritual, but we intuit that there must be a purpose for "all this" and decide to make an attempt at figuring things out.

This goes on for some lives, until in one life we begin looking inward, feeling that "something" must be there to find. After a number of more lives, trying this and that in our search, we have the good karma to discover an actual spiritual methodology that will reveal what we are seeking if we apply it correctly and diligently. In other words: we learn yoga and become a yogi.

"Plowing" the field through yoga practice, according to our persistence and fervor we eventually find the treasure–the Self. And we not only "see" it, we possess it and identify with it fully. That is, we come to know the Self and thereby know God.

He began to lend money at interest to whomever he wished. Having found the treasure we share it with others whom we feel are truly interested and capable of finding the Self. The "interest" exacted of them is faithful practice and the conforming of their life to the yogic principles of yama and niyama. In time they, too, gain the treasure hidden in their field and can also share it with others as we shared with them.

And so the story ends as Eternity begins.

"Therefore, become a yogi" (Bhagavad Gita 6:46).

HAVING COME TO THE END

Jesus said, Whoever finds the world and becomes rich, let him renounce the world. (110)

What we see all around us is an illusion. The essence of everything is Divine Light–God himself. To truly "find" something is to find its real nature, its Self. God is the Self of the world, and whoever finds God is rich indeed because God is everything and even more: Transcendent Infinity. So he who finds the world finds the totality of Being. When that is found he should deny and renounce the world as he formerly saw it. Then he must affirm and relate to the world in a divine manner. Rejecting the world because of apparent faults is no wisdom at all; but renouncing the false impressions of the world and affirming the truth of its nature is the highest wisdom.

IMMORTAL AND
ABOVE THE WORLD

Jesus said, The heavens and the earth will be rolled up in your presence. And the one who lives from the living one will not see death. Does not Jesus say, Whoever finds himself is superior to the world? (111)

> *Patterson and Maeyer:* The heavens and the earth will roll up in your presence, and whoever is living from the living one will not see death. Does not Jesus say, Those who have found themselves, of them the world is not worthy?

The heavens and the earth will be rolled up in your presence. Creation occurs in cycles. Here it is likened to a scroll that is unrolled and rolled up, and all the sentient beings are subject to it. The Bhagavad Gita explains it very well:

"They know the true day and night who know Brahma's Day a thousand yugas long and Brahma's Night a thousand yugas long. At the approach of Brahma's Day, all manifested things come forth from the unmanifest, and then return to that at Brahma's Night. Helpless, the same host of beings being born again and again merge at the approach of the Night and emerge at the dawn of Day.

"But there exists, higher than the unmanifested, another unmanifested Eternal which does not perish when all beings perish. This unmanifest is declared to be the imperishable, which is called the Supreme Goal, attaining which they return not. This is my supreme abode. This is the Supreme Being, attained by one-pointed devotion alone, within which all beings do dwell, by which all this is pervaded" (Bhagavad Gita 8:17-22).

The one who lives from the living one will not see death. In Mahayana Buddhism they often speak of the need for good roots. In this verse the idea is that he who is rooted consciously in the Supreme Immortal will never experience death, and so will have nothing to fear at the dissolution of the cosmos.

Whoever finds himself is superior to the world. He who comes to know himself in the enlightenment known as Self-realization is superior to the world for he is no longer subject to coming and going, to birth and death. He is not compelled to come forth at the day of creation nor to be withdrawn at its night.

"Whatever meritorious fruit is declared to accrue from study or recitation of the Vedas, sacrifice, tapasya, and almsgiving–beyond all these goes the yogi who knows the two paths [the one that leads to rebirth and the one that leads beyond rebirth]; and he attains to the supreme, primeval Abode" (Bhagavad Gita 8:28).

BODY AND SOUL

Jesus said, Woe to the flesh that depends on the soul; woe to the soul that depends on the flesh. (112)

"Flesh" means the physical body, the *sarx*; and "soul" means the subtle energy body or bodies, the *psyche*. The flesh cannot depend on the soul because they are intertwined, being formed of energy, and sharing the same weaknesses and defects. And for the same reason the soul, especially the mind, cannot depend on the body because it is trapped in the body and continually subject to its changes and conditions.

What Jesus is implying is that both flesh and body need the spirit, the *pneuma*, because it alone is immortal and its nature is consciousness. Just as God projects the creation out of his own unchanging Consciousness, in the same way the bodies, including the physical body, have emanated from the individual spirit. Therefore both flesh and soul must be aligned or attuned to the spirit and eventually absorbed into the spirit which is their goal. Until then, through spiritual practice, especially meditation, both flesh and soul must be always oriented to the spirit which is itself part of the Divine.

WHERE IS THE KINGDOM?

His disciples said to him, When will the kingdom come?
[Jesus said,] It will not come by waiting for it. It will not be
a matter of saying 'here it is' or 'there it is.' Rather, the kingdom
of the father is spread out upon the earth, and men do not see
it. (113)

> *Brill:* It cometh not with observation. They will not say: Lo, here!
> or: Lo, there! But the kingdom of the Father is spread out upon
> the earth, and men do not see it.

It will not come by waiting for it. If we wait to see the kingdom coming, as nearly all prophecy-obsessed Christians do, it will never arrive. For two thousand years people have been claiming (and on occasion "proving") that the return of Jesus is immanent and that the establishment of the kingdom of God on earth is near—even though Jesus said: "My kingdom is not of this world" (John 18:36).

It will not be a matter of saying "here it is" or "there it is." By this Jesus is saying that we will not have to go somewhere to find the kingdom, that it will not at all be a matter of "come over here" or "go over there." It will not be a matter of the kingdom being in one place and not in another.

Rather, the kingdom of the father is spread out upon the earth, and men do not see it. The kingdom is here right now throughout the world, but it is invisible–at least to human eyes, but not to the eyes of those evolving beyond ordinary humanity. So we need not go anywhere to find the kingdom. We need only open the wisdom eye of the spirit and see ourselves as we truly are: the divine, immortal Self. For the Self is the kingdom–as is God, the Self of the Self.

MALE AND FEMALE?

Simon Peter said to him, Let Mary leave us, for women are not worthy of life.

Jesus said, I myself shall lead her in order to make her male, so that she too may become a living spirit resembling you males. For every woman who will make herself male will enter the kingdom of heaven. (114)

I sometimes wonder if Saint Thomas left this for the last because of the gross stupidity of the first sentence and the need to combat it. Even today in India there are people who believe that there is no need for a woman to engage in meditation because it is impossible for a woman to attain liberation.

My friend, Saguna Hejmadi (a cousin of Swami–"Papa"–Ramdas of Anandashram), was once at the Anandamayi Ashram in New Delhi (Kalkaji). Somehow an ignoramus standing nearby learned that she was a disciple of Ma Anandamayi and did a great deal of meditation. "Why are you wasting your time with all that?" he asked, "women cannot attain liberation–only men can attain liberation." Foolishly she began arguing with the the man, who bolstered his assertions with many scriptural quotes. In the midst of this altercation, Anandamayi Ma came walking through the room. "MA!" called out Saguna, "Is it true that women cannot attain liberation?" Still walking on, Ma nodded and answered: "That is true. Women cannot attain liberation." Saguna stood there completely thunderstruck as the man chuckled and chortled at his "triumph." After standing and stewing for nearly half an hour, Saguna saw Ma returning. Ma came right up to her, said: "And men do not attain liberation either!" and walked on and out of the room. Then Saguna understood: only those who transcend body identity and live identified with the spirit-self can attain liberation.

One of India's greatest yogis, Paramhansa Nityananda, had this to say in section 61 of *The Chidakasha Gita*: "Now the distinction of male and female. A true female is one who is merged in the external; a true male is one who is merged in the internal. One whose buddhi is firm is male; one whose buddhi is fickle is a female. This distinction of male and female is external only. Internally such a distinction does not exist at all. When the manas and buddhi are merged in the atman, one who is physically a woman becomes spiritually a man."

And so the great yogi has explained Jesus' words far better than I ever could.

In Conclusion

The first sentence in this book was: "From the very beginning there were two Christianities." And now we have certainly seen that this is true.

If you wish to pursue the matter further, I recommend that you obtain and study *The Nag Hammadi Library*, a collection of very ancient Christian texts, and *The Odes of Solomon*, a collection of the earliest Christian hymns.

Especially valuable is a modern book, *The Aquarian Gospel of Jesus the Christ*, a record of the psychic impressions of Reverend Levi Dowling regarding the life and teachings of Jesus. In my opinion this is the only book which contains the true account of Jesus' life and teaching.

I would also like to recommend *The Second Coming of Christ* by Paramhansa Yogananda, which is his commentary on the Gospels.

GLOSSARY

Agni: Vedic god of fire.

Bhagavad Gita: "The Song of God." The sacred philosophical text often called "the Hindu Bible," part of the epic Mahabharata by Vyasa; the most popular sacred text in Hinduism.

Bhagavan: The Lord; the One endowed with the six attributes, viz. infinite treasures, strength, glory, splendor knowledge, and renunciation; the Personal God.

Brahman: The Absolute Reality; the Truth proclaimed in the Upanishads; the Supreme Reality that is one and indivisible, infinite, and eternal; all-pervading, changeless Existence; Existence-knowledge-bliss Absolute (Satchidananda); Absolute Consciousness; it is not only all-powerful but all-power itself; not only all-knowing and blissful but all-knowledge and all-bliss itself.

Chidakasha: "The Space (Ether) of Consciousness." The infinite, all-pervading expanse of Consciousness from which all "things" proceed; the subtle space of Consciousness in the Sahasrara (Thousand-petalled Lotus). The true "heart" of all things.

Chinmaya: Full of consciousnes; formed of consciousness.

Gerua: The brownish-orange mud used to dye the clothing of Hindu monastics; the color produced by dyeing with gerua is also called gerua.

Gopis: The milkmaids of Vrindavan, companions and devotees of Krishna.

Maya: The illusive power of Brahman; the veiling and the projecting power of the universe, the power of Cosmic Illusion. "The Measurer"–a reference to the two delusive "measures": Time and Space.

Paramahan[m]sa/Paramhan[m]sa: Literally: Supreme Swan, a person of the highest spiritual realization, from the fact that a swan can separate milk from water and is therefore an apt symbol for one who has discarded the unreal for the Real, the darkness for the Light, and mortality for the Immortal, having separated himself fully from all that is not God and joined himself totally to the Divine, becoming a veritable embodiment of Divinity manifested in humanity.

Prakriti: Causal matter; the fundamental power (shakti) of God from which the entire cosmos is formed; the root base of all elements; undifferentiated matter; the material cause of the world. Also known as Pradhana.

Prana: Life; vital energy; life-breath; life-force; inhalation. In the human body the prana is divided into five forms: 1) Prana, the prana that moves upward; 2) Apana: The prana that moves downward, producing the excretory functions in general. 3) Vyana: The prana that holds prana and apana together and produces circulation in the body. 4) Samana: The prana that carries the grosser material of food to the apana and brings the subtler material to each limb; the general force of digestion. 5) Udana: The prana which brings up or carries down what has been drunk or eaten; the general force of assimilation.

Purusha: "Person" in the sense of a conscious spirit. Both God and the individual spirits are purushas, but God is the Adi (Original, Archetypal) Purusha, Parama (Highest) Purusha, and the Purushottama (Highest or Best of the Purushas).

Samsara: Life through repeated births and deaths; the wheel of birth and death; the process of earthly life.

Sanatana Dharma: "The Eternal Religion," also known as "Arya Dharma," "the religion of those who strive upward [Aryas]." Hinduism.

Satchidananda: Existence-Knowledge-Bliss Absolute; Brahman.

Satsanga: Literally: "company with Truth." Association with god-ly-minded persons. The company of saints and devotees.

Shankara: Shankaracharya; Adi (the first) Shankaracharya: The great reformer and re-establisher of Vedic Religion in India around 300 B.C. He is the unparalleled exponent of Advaita (Non-Dual) Vedanta. He also reformed the mode of monastic life and founded (or regenerated) the ancient Swami Order.

Shiva: A name of God meaning "One Who is all Bliss and the giver of happiness to all." Although classically applied to the Absolute Brahman, Shiva can also refer to God (Ishwara) in His aspect of Dissolver and Liberator (often mistakenly thought of as "destroyer").

Swayamprakash(a): Self-luminous; self-illumined.

Tapasya: Austerity; practical (i.e., result-producing) spiritual discipline; spiritual force. Literally it means the generation of heat or energy, but is always used in a symbolic manner, referring to spiritual practice and its effect, especially the roasting of karmic seeds, the burning up of karma.

Upanishads: Books (of varying lengths) of the philosophical teachings of the ancient sages of India on the knowledge of Absolute Reality. The upanishads contain two major themes: (1) the individual self (atman) and the Supreme Self (Paramatman) are one in essence, and (2) the goal of life is the realization/manifestation of this unity, the realization of God (Brahman). There are eleven principal upanishads: Isha, Kena, Katha, Prashna, Mundaka, Mandukya, Taittiriya, Aitareya, Chandogya, Brihadaranyaka, and Shvetashvatara, all of which were commented on by Shankara, Ramanuja and Madhavacharya, thus setting the seal of authenticity on them.

Vedas: The oldest scriptures of India, considered the oldest scriptures of the world, that were revealed in meditation to the Vedic Rishis (seers). Although in modern times there are said to be four Vedas (Rig, Sama, Yajur, and Atharva), in the upanishads only three are listed (Rig, Sama, and Yajur). In actuality, there is only one Veda: the Rig Veda. The Sama Veda is only a collection of Rig Veda hymns that are marked (pointed) for singing. The Yajur Veda is a small book giving directions on just one form of Vedic sacrifice. The Atharva Veda is only a collection of theurgical mantras to be recited for the cure of various afflictions or to be recited over the herbs to be taken as medicine for those afflictions.

DID YOU ENJOY READING THIS BOOK?

Thank you for taking the time to read *The Gospel of Thomas for Awakening*. If you enjoyed it, please consider telling your friends or posting a short review at Amazon.com, Goodreads, or the online site of your choice.

Word of mouth is an author's best friend and much appreciated.

GET YOUR FREE MEDITATION GUIDE

Sign up for the Light of the Spirit Newsletter and get
Learn How to Meditate Effectively.

Get free updates: newsletters, blog posts, and podcasts, plus exclusive content from Light of the Spirit Monastery.

Visit: https://ocoy.org/signup

ABOUT THE AUTHOR

Swami Nirmalananda Giri (Abbot George Burke) is the founder and director of the Light of the Spirit Monastery (Atma Jyoti Ashram) in Cedar Crest, New Mexico, USA.

In his many pilgrimages to India, he had the opportunity of meeting some of India's greatest spiritual figures, including Swami Sivananda of Rishikesh and Anandamayi Ma. During his first trip to India he was made a member of the ancient Swami Order by Swami Vidyananda Giri, a direct disciple of Paramhansa Yogananda, who had himself been given sannyas by the Shankaracharya of Puri, Jagadguru Bharati Krishna Tirtha.

In the United States he also encountered various Christian saints, including Saint John Maximovich of San Francisco and Saint Philaret Voznesensky of New York. He was ordained in the Liberal Catholic Church (International) to the priesthood on January 25, 1974, and consecrated a bishop on August 23, 1975.

For many years Swami Nirmalananda has researched the identity of Jesus Christ and his teachings with India and Sanatana Dharma, including Yoga. It is his conclusion that Jesus lived in India for most of his life, and was a yogi and Sanatana Dharma missionary to the West. After his resurrection he returned to India and lived the rest of his life in the Himalayas.

He has written extensively on these and other topics, many of which are posted at OCOY.org.

ATMA JYOTI ASHRAM
(LIGHT OF THE SPIRIT MONASTERY)

Atma Jyoti Ashram (Light of the Spirit Monastery) is a monastic community for those men who seek direct experience of the Spirit through yoga meditation, traditional yogic discipline, Sanatana Dharma and the life of the sannyasi in the tradition of the Order of Shankara. Our lineage is in the Giri branch of the Order.

The public outreach of the monastery is through its website, OCOY.org (Original Christianity and Original Yoga). There you will find many articles on Original Christianity and Original Yoga, including *The Christ of India*. *Foundations of Yoga* and *How to Be a Yogi* are practical guides for anyone seriously interested in living the Yoga Life.

You will also discover many other articles on leading an effective spiritual life, including *Soham Yoga: The Yoga of the Self* and *Spiritual Benefits of a Vegetarian Diet*, as well as the "Dharma for Awakening" series–in-depth commentaries on these spiritual classics: the Bhagavad Gita, the Upanishads, the Dhammapada, the Tao Teh King and more.

You can listen to podcasts by Swami Nirmalananda on meditation, the Yoga Life, and remarkable spiritual people he has met in India and elsewhere, at http://ocoy.org/podcasts/

Reading for Awakening

Light of the Spirit Press presents books on spiritual wisdom and Original Christianity and Original Yoga. From our "Dharma for Awakening" series (practical commentaries on the world's scriptures) to books on how to meditate and live a successful spiritual life, you will find books that are informative, helpful, and even entertaining.

Light of the Spirit Press is the publishing house of Light of the Spirit Monastery (Atma Jyoti Ashram) in Cedar Crest, New Mexico, USA. Our books feature the writings of the founder and director of the monastery, Swami Nirmalananda Giri (Abbot George Burke) which are also found on the monastery's website, OCOY.org.

We invite you to explore our publications in the following pages.

Find out more about our publications at
lightofthespiritpress.com

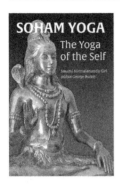

Soham Yoga
The Yoga of the Self

A complete and in-depth guide to effective meditation and the life that supports it, this important book explains with clarity and insight what real yoga is, and why and how to practice Soham Yoga meditation.

Discovered centuries ago by the Nath yogis, this simple and classic approach to self-realization has no "secrets," requires no "initiation," and is easily accessible to the serious modern yogi.

Includes helpful, practical advice on leading an effective spiritual life and many Illuminating quotes on Soham from Indian scriptures and great yogis.

"This book is a complete spiritual path." –Arnold Van Wie

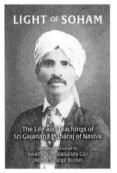

Light of Soham
The Life and Teachings of Sri Gajanana Maharaj of Nashik

Gajanan Murlidhar Gupte, later known as Gajanana Maharaj, led an unassuming life, to all appearances a normal unmarried man of contemporary society. Crediting his personal transformation to the practice of the Soham mantra, he freely shared this practice with a small number of disciples, whom he simply called his friends. Strictly avoiding the trap of gurudom, he insisted that his friends be self-reliant and not be dependent on him for their spiritual progress. Yet he was uniquely able to assist them in their inner development.

The Inspired Wisdom of Gajanana Maharaj
A Practical Commentary on Leading an Effectual Spiritual Life

Presents the teachings and sayings of the great twentieth-century Soham yogi Gajanana Maharaj, with a commentary by Swami Nirmalananda.

The author writes: "In reading about Gajanana Maharaj I encountered a holy personality that eclipsed all others for me. In his words I found a unique wisdom that altered my perspective on what yoga, yogis, and gurus should be.

"But I realized that through no fault of their own, many Western readers need a clarification and expansion of Maharaj's meaning to get the right understanding of his words. This commentary is meant to help my friends who, like me have found his words 'a light in the darkness.'"

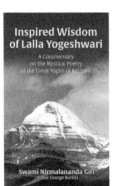

Inspired Wisdom of Lalla Yogeshwari
A Commentary on the Mystical Poetry of the Great Yogini of Kashmir

Lalla Yogeshwari was a great fourteenth-century yogini and wandering ascetic of Kashmir, whose mystic poetry were the earliest compositions in the Kashmiri language. She was in the tradition of the Nath Yogi Sampradaya whose meditation practice is that of Soham Sadhana: the joining of the mental repetition of Soham Mantra with the natural breath.

Swami Nirmalananda's commentary mines the treasures of Lalleshwari's mystic poems and presents his reflections in an easily intelligible fashion for those wishing to put these priceless teachings on the path of yogic self-transformation into practice.

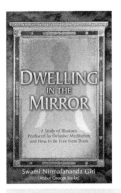

Dwelling in the Mirror
*A Study of Illusions Produced By Delusive Meditation
And How to Be Free from Them*

Swami Nirmalananda says of this book:
"Over and over people have mistaken trivial and pathological conditions for enlightenment, written books, given seminars and gained a devoted following.
"Most of these unfortunate people were completely unreachable with reason. Yet there are those who can have an experience and realize that it really cannot be real, but a vagary of their mind. Some may not understand that on their own, but can be shown by others the truth about it. For them and those that may one day be in danger of meditation-produced delusions I have written this brief study."

BOOKS ON YOGA & SPIRITUAL LIFE

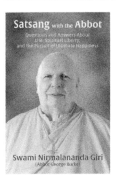

Satsang with the Abbot
*Questions and Answers about Life, Spiritual Liberty,
and the Pursuit of Ultimate Happiness*

The questions in this book range from the most sublime to the most practical. "How can I attain samadhi?" "I am married with children. How can I lead a spiritual life?" "What is Self-realization?" "How important is belief in karma and reincarnation?"
In Swami Nirmalananda's replies to these questions the reader will discover common sense, helpful information, and a guiding light for their journey through and beyond the forest of cliches, contradictions, and confusion of yoga, Hinduism, Christianity, and metaphysical thought.

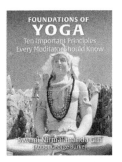

Foundations of Yoga
Ten Important Principles Every Meditator Should Know

An introduction to the important foundation principles of Patanjali's Yoga: Yama and Niyama
Yama and Niyama are often called the Ten Commandments of Yoga, but they have nothing to do with the ideas of sin and virtue or good and evil as dictated by some cosmic potentate. Rather they are determined by a thoroughly practical, pragmatic basis: that which strengthens and facilitates our yoga practice should be observed and that which weakens or hinders it should be avoided.

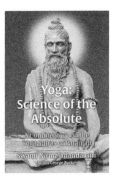

Yoga: Science of the Absolute
A Commentary on the Yoga Sutras of Patanjali

The Yoga Sutras of Patanjali is the most authoritative text on Yoga as a practice. It is also known as the Yoga Darshana because it is the fundamental text of Yoga as a philosophy.
In this commentary, Swami Nirmalananda draws on the age-long tradition regarding this essential text, including the commentaries of Vyasa and Shankara, the most highly regarded writers on Indian philosophy and practice, as well as I. K. Taimni and other authoritative commentators, and adds his own ideas based on half a century of study and practice. Serious students of yoga will find this an essential addition to their spiritual studies.

The Benefits of Brahmacharya
A Collection of Writings About the Spiritual, Mental, and Physical Benefits of Continence

"Brahmacharya is the basis for morality. It is the basis for eternal life. It is a spring flower that exhales immortality from its petals." Swami Sivananda

This collection of articles from a variety of authorities including Mahatma Gandhi, Sri Ramakrishna, Swami Vivekananda, Swamis Sivananda and Chidananda of the Divine Life Society, Swami Nirmalananda, and medical experts, presents many facets of brahmacharya and will prove of immense value to all who wish to grow spiritually.

Living the Yoga Life
Perspectives on Yoga

"Dive deep; otherwise you cannot get the gems at the bottom of the ocean. You cannot pick up the gems if you only float on the surface." Sri Ramakrishna

In *Living the Yoga Life* Swami Nirmalananda shares the gems he has found from a lifetime of "diving deep." This collection of reflections and short essays addresses the key concepts of yoga philosophy that are so easy to take for granted. Never content with the accepted cliches about yoga sadhana, the yoga life, the place of a guru, the nature of Brahman and our unity with It, Swami Nirmalananda's insights on these and other facets of the yoga life will inspire, provoke, enlighten, and even entertain.

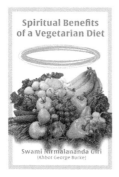

Spiritual Benefits of a Vegetarian Diet

The health benefits of a vegetarian diet are well known, as are the ethical aspects. But the spiritual advantages should be studied by anyone involved in meditation, yoga, or any type of spiritual practice.

Diet is a crucial aspect of emotional, intellectual, and spiritual development as well. For diet and consciousness are interrelated, and purity of diet is an effective aid to purity and clarity of consciousness.

The major thing to keep in mind when considering the subject of vegetarianism is its relevancy in relation to our explorations of consciousness. We need only ask: Does it facilitate my spiritual growth–the development and expansion of my consciousness? The answer is Yes.

BOOKS ON THE SACRED SCRIPTURES OF INDIA

The Bhagavad Gita for Awakening
A Practical Commentary for Leading a Successful Spiritual Life

Drawing from the teachings of Sri Ramakrishna, Jesus, Paramhansa Yogananda, Ramana Maharshi, Swami Vivekananda, Swami Sivananda of Rishikesh, Papa Ramdas, and other spiritual masters and teachers, as well as his own experiences, Swami Nirmalananda illustrates the teachings of the Gita with stories which make the teachings of Krishna in the Gita vibrant and living.

From *Publisher's Weekly*: "[The author] enthusiastically explores the story as a means for knowing oneself, the cosmos, and one's calling within it. His plainspoken insights often distill complex lessons with simplicity and sagacity. Those with a deep interest in the Gita will find much wisdom here."

The Upanishads for Awakening
A Practical Commentary on India's Classical Scriptures

The sacred scriptures of India are vast. Yet they are only different ways of seeing the same thing, the One Thing which makes them both valid and ultimately harmonious. That unifying subject is Brahman: God the Absolute, beyond and besides whom there is no "other" whatsoever. The thirteen major Upanishads are the fountainhead of all expositions of Brahman.

Swami Nirmalananda illumines the Upanishads' practical value for spiritual seekers from the unique perspective of a lifetime of study and practice of both Eastern and Western spirituality.

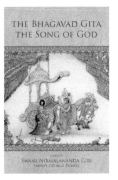

The Bhagavad Gita–The Song of God

Often called the "Bible" of Hinduism, the Bhagavad Gita is found in households throughout India and has been translated into every major language of the world. Literally billions of copies have been handwritten or printed.

The clarity of this translation by Swami Nirmalananda makes for easy reading, while the rich content makes this the ideal "study" Gita. As the original Sanskrit language is so rich, often there are several accurate translations for the same word, which are noted in the text, giving the spiritual student the needed understanding of the fullness of the Gita.

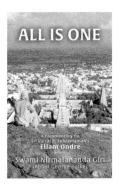

All Is One
A Commentary On Sri Vaiyai R. Subramanian's Ellam Ondre

"I you want moksha, read and practice the instructions in Ellam Ondre."
–Ramana Maharshi

Swami Nirmalananda's insightful commentary brings even further light to Ellam Ondre's refreshing perspective on what Unity signifies, and the path to its realization.

Written in the colorful and well-informed style typical of his other commentaries, it is a timely and important contribution to Advaitic literature that explains Unity as the fruit of yoga sadhana, rather than mere wishful thinking or some vague intellectual gymnastic, as is so commonly taught by the modern "Advaita gurus."

A Brief Sanskrit Glossary
A Spiritual Student's Guide to Essential Sanskrit Terms

This Sanskrit glossary contains full translations and explanations of hundreds of the most commonly used spiritual Sanskrit terms, and will help students of the Bhagavad Gita, the Upanishads, the Yoga Sutras of Patanjali, and other Indian scriptures and philosophical works to expand their vocabularies to include the Sanskrit terms contained in these, and gain a fuller understanding in their studies.

The Christ of India
The Story of Original Christianity

"Original Christianity" is the teaching of both Jesus and his Apostle Saint Thomas in India. Although it was new to the Mediterranean world, it was really the classical, traditional teachings of the rishis of India that even today comprise the Eternal Dharma, that goes far beyond religion into realization.

In *The Christ of India* Swami Nirmalananda presents what those ancient teachings are, as well as the growing evidence that Jesus spent much of his "Lost Years" in India and Tibet. This is also the story of how the original teachings of Jesus and Saint Thomas thrived in India for centuries before the coming of the European colonialists.

May a Christian Believe in Reincarnation?

Discover the real and surprising history of reincarnation and Christianity.

A growing number of people are open to the subject of past lives, and the belief in rebirth–reincarnation, metempsychosis, or transmigration–is commonplace. It often thought that belief in reincarnation and Christianity are incompatible. But is this really true? May a Christian believe in reincarnation? The answer may surprise you.

"Those needing evidence that a belief in reincarnation is in accordance with teachings of the Christ need look no further: Plainly laid out and explained in an intelligent manner from one who has spent his life on a Christ-like path of renunciation and prayer/meditation."—Christopher T. Cook

The Unknown Lives of Jesus and Mary
Compiled from Ancient Records and Mystical Revelations

"There are also many other things which Jesus did, the which, if they should be written every one, I suppose that even the world itself could not contain the books that should be written." (Gospel of Saint John, final verse)

You can discover much of those "many other things" in this unique compilation of ancient records and mystical revelations, which includes historical records of the lives of Jesus Christ and his Mother Mary that have been accepted and used by the Church since apostolic times. This treasury of little-known stories of Jesus' life will broaden the reader's understanding of what Christianity really was in its original form.

Robe of Light
An Esoteric Christian Cosmology

In *Robe of Light* Swami Nirmalananda explores the whys and wherefores of the mystery of creation. From the emanation of the worlds from the very Being of God, to the evolution of the souls to their ultimate destiny as perfected Sons of God, the ideal progression of creation is described. Since the rebellion of Lucifer and the fall of Adam and Eve from Paradise flawed the normal plan of evolution, a restoration was necessary. How this came about is the prime subject of this insightful study.

Moreover, what this means to aspirants for spiritual perfection is expounded, with a compelling knowledge of the scriptures and of the mystical traditions of East and West.

The Gospel of Thomas for Awakening
A Commentary on Jesus' Sayings as Recorded by the Apostle Thomas

When the Apostles dispersed to the various area of the world, Thomas travelled to India, where evidence shows Jesus spent his Lost Years, and which had been the source of the wisdom which he had brought to the "West."

The Christ that Saint Thomas quotes in this ancient text is quite different than the Christ presented by popular Christianity. Through his unique experience and study with both Christianity and Indian religion, Swami Nirmalananda clarifies the sometimes enigmatic sayings of Jesus in an informative and inspiring way.

The Odes of Solomon for Awakening
A Commentary on the Mystical Wisdom of the
Earliest Christian Hymns and Poems

The Odes of Solomon is the earliest Christian hymn-book, and therefore one of the most important early Christian documents. Since they are mystical and esoteric, they teach and express the classical and universal mystical truths of Christianity, revealing a Christian perspective quite different than that of "Churchianity," and present the path of Christhood that all Christians are called to.

"Fresh and soothing, these 41 poems and hymns are beyond delightful! I deeply appreciate Abbot George Burke's useful and illuminating insight and find myself spiritually re-animated." –John Lawhn

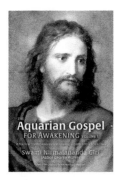

The Aquarian Gospel for Awakening (2 Volumes)
A Practical Commentary on Levi Dowling's Classic Life of Jesus Christ

Written in 1908 by the American mystic Levi Dowling, The Aquarian Gospel of Jesus the Christ answers many questions about Jesus' life that the Bible doesn't address. Dowling presents a universal message found at the heart of all valid religions, a broad vision of love and wisdom that will ring true with Christians who are attracted to Christ but put off by the narrow views of the tradition that has been given his name.

Swami Nirmalananda's commentary is a treasure-house of knowledge and insight that even further expands Dowling's vision of the true Christ and his message.

Wandering With The Cherubim
A Commentary on the Mystical Verse of Angelus
Silesius–The Cherubinic Wanderer"

Johannes Scheffler, who wrote under the name Angelus Silesius, was a mystic and a poet. In his most famous book, "The Cherubinic Wanderer," he expressed his mystical vision.

Swami Nirmalananda reveals the timelessness of his mystical teachings and The Cherubinic Wanderer's practical value for spiritual seekers. He does this in an easily intelligible fashion for those wishing to put those priceless teachings into practice.

"Set yourself on the journey of this mystical poetry made accessible through this very beautifully commentated text. It is text that submerges one in the philosophical context of the Advaita notion of Non Duality. Swami Nirmalananda's commentary is indispensable in understanding higher philosophical ideas, for Swami's language, while readily approachable, is rich in deep essence of the teachings." –Savitri

The Dhammapada for Awakening
A Commentary on Buddha's Practical Wisdom

Swami Nirmalananda's commentary on this classic Buddhist scripture explores the Buddha's answers to the urgent questions, such as "How can I find find lasting peace, happiness and fulfillment that seems so elusive?" and "What can I do to avoid many of the miseries big and small that afflict all of us?" Drawing on his personal experience and on parallels in Hinduism and Christianity, the author sheds new light on the Buddha's eternal wisdom.

"Swami Nirmalananda's commentary is well crafted and stacked with anecdotes, humor, literary references and beautiful quotes from the Buddha. I found it to be entertaining as well as illuminating, and have come to consider it a guide to daily living." –Rev. Gerry Nangle

The Tao Teh King for Awakening
A Practical Commentary on Lao Tzu's Classic Exposition of Taoism

"The Tao does all things, yet our interior disposition determines our success or failure in coming to knowledge of the unknowable Tao."

Lao Tzu's classic writing, the Tao Teh King, has fascinated scholars and seekers for centuries. His presentation of the Tao which is the Eternal Reality, and the Way of the Sage that is the path to the realization of and dwelling in this Reality is illuminating, but its deeper meanings and practical applications remain obscure to many, especially in the West.

Swami Nirmalananda offers a commentary that makes the treasures of Lao Tzu's teachings accessible and applicable for the sincere seeker.

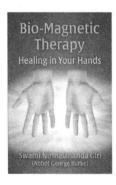

Bio-Magnetic Therapy
Healing in Your Hands

In *Bio-Magnetic Therapy* Swami Nirmalananda teaches the techniques to strengthen your vitality and improve the body's natural healing ability in yourself and in others with specific methods that anyone can use.

Bio-Magnetic Therapy is a simple and natural way to increase the flow of life-force into the body for general good health and to stimulate the supply and flow of life-force to a troubled area that has become vitality-starved through some obstruction. It does not cure; it simply aids the body to cure itself by supplying it with curative force.

More Titles
The Four Gospels for Awakening
Light on the Path for Awakening
How to Read the Tarot
Light from Eternal Lamps
Vivekachudamani: The Crest Jewel of Discrimination for Awakening
Sanatana Dharma: The Eternal Religion